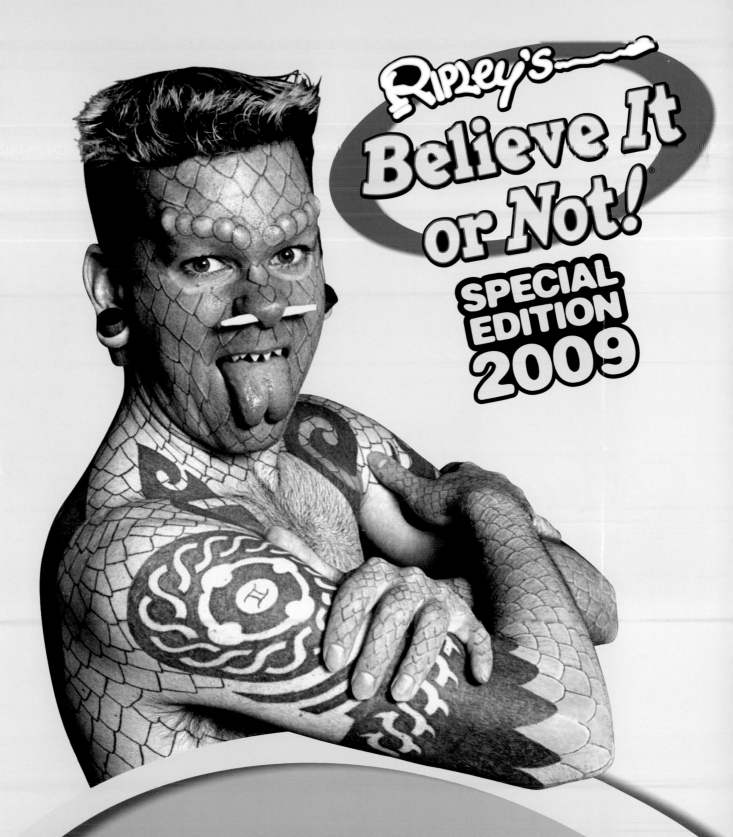

Ripley's Believe It or Not!
SPECIAL EDITION 2009

SCHOLASTIC INC.

New York   Toronto   London   Auckland   Sydney
Mexico City   New Delhi   Hong Kong   Buenos Aires

Library of Congress Cataloging-in-Publication data is available

ISBN-13: 978-0-545-07705-7
ISBN-10: 0-545-07705-2

PUBLISHING

Developed and produced by Miles Kelly Publishing Ltd
in association with Ripley Publishing

Publishing Director: Anne Marshall
Art Director: Sam South
Managing Editor: Becky Miles

Project Editor: Rosie Alexander
Picture Manager: Gemma Simmons
Editorial Assistant: Charlotte Marshall
Designer: Rachel Cross
Indexer: Hilary Bird
Reprographics: Stephan Davis

12 11 10 9 8 7 6 5 4 3 2 1   8 9 10 11 12/0

Printed in China

First printing, September 2008

CONTENTS

Introduction - Robert Ripley ● 4

Chapter 1 - Way-Out World ● 8

Chapter 2 - Flaky Folk ● 30

Chapter 3 - Animal Antics ● 52

Chapter 4 - Against the Odds ● 74

Chapter 5 - Body Oddity ● 96

Chapter 6 - Strange but True ● 118

Index .... ● 140

Photo Credits .... ● 144

ROBERT RIPLEY

In 1918, while working for the *New York Globe*, Robert Ripley hit upon the idea of drawing cartoons that featured the planet's wonders, miracles, and almost-impossible feats. The result: a column entitled *Believe It or Not!* which ultimately had a worldwide readership of 80 million people, and a mailbox spilling over with 3,500 letters a day!

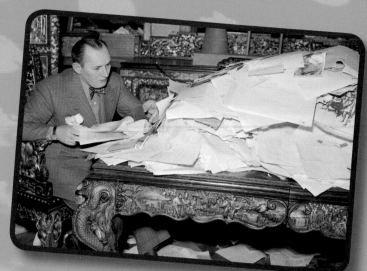

MAN-EATING TREE

"BULUM BALUBA" from Ripley
SUVA, FIJI ISLANDS

weird and wonderful

It was the start of the Ripley phenomenon. By 1940, he had visited no fewer than 201 countries, totaling an amazing 464,000 miles—equivalent to 18 times round the equator, or more than the distance from the Earth to the Moon and back. Year after year, mile after mile, he hunted and gathered for his column.

The weirdest and most wonderful of the thousands of facts he collected were exhibited in Ripley museums known as "odditoriums." When Chicago's museum opened in 1933, 100 people a day fainted at the sight of its weirdities — six beds were on hand to cope. So be prepared!

Sometimes the features in this book will seem too strange to be true. Robert Ripley was often dubbed a liar, to which he responded, "There's nothing stranger than the truth." On these pages, every fascinating fact and bizarre behavior is genuine. Welcome to the wonderful world we live in!

Oh No, Overdrawn Again, page 71

Worm Squirm, page 49

Board Out of His Mind, page 76

Ripley Rewind

Ripley's has a massive database of weird facts and a giant-sized library of photographs. Robert Ripley drew inspiration for his cartoons from these black and white photos, some of which appear in the Ripley Rewind features in this book. Here is the photo that appears on page 35, with the cartoon Ripley drew for the *New York Globe*.

MRS. ANNA EDSON TAYLOR
THE FIRST TO SURVIVE GOING OVER NIAGARA FALLS IN A BARREL, STAGED THE FEAT IN 1901 NOT FOR GLORY BUT **TO PAY THE INTEREST ON HER TEXAS RANCH**

Fall Girl

In 1901, Annie Edson Taylor was the first person to survive going over Niagara Falls in a barrel. She was in the barrel for 1 hour 15 minutes before being rescued.

The Last Word

If you enjoy jaw-dropping information, soak up the extra 20 facts on the Last Word pages found at the end of each chapter. Then take a look at the Math Path challenge on pages 138–139 to test how well you know this book.

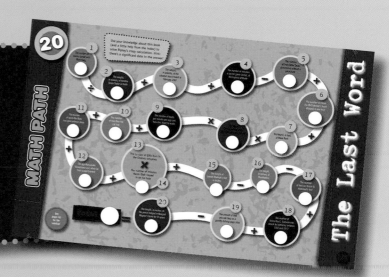

Ripley Reward

Keep an eye out for the special Ripley Reward. It's been presented to a feature that is particularly worthy of note. Rest assured, it'll be very weird, very Ripley.

Toastermobile

American Bob Blumer has an unusual method of cooking, preferring a car engine to an oven! After wrapping meat and fish in aluminum foil, Bob cooks the food on the engine of his "Toastermobile"—a trailer complete with professional kitchen and two eight-foot-high slices of toast.

the surreal gourmet

the surreal gourmet

Chapter 1
WAY OUT WORLD

WE'RE ROCKING

Time for a Cut

It's not the hair of a rock star—but a hairy head of rock! Uncovered in China in 2004, this rare-hair stone, measuring 6 x 8 inches, is covered with a growing fungus, according to marine experts. It comes at a price of around $1½ million!

What on Earth?

There's no pot of gold at the end of this rainbow, but the seven colored layers of earth at Chamerel, on the island of Mauritius in the Indian Ocean, attract visitors from all over the world. Even when the colors of these dunes of mineral-rich volcanic ash get mixed together during heavy rains, the red, brown, violet, green, blue, purple, and yellow layers separate again after a few days!

Rock-a-doodle-do

Strutting its stuff, the image of a rooster occurs naturally on this stone found in Anhui, China, in 2001. In China, there is a centuries-old tradition of collecting odd stones—to admire, to touch, to trade, or just to talk to like pet rocks! Other stone images found there include flowers, fish, and famous heads.

Solid Surf

Imagine a gigantic wave of water frozen in time in the middle of a dry desert! Welcome to the Wave Rock in Hyden, Western Australia, with a "surf" over 45 feet high and more than 350 feet long. Its face was shaped by erosion long before the dinosaurs—longer still before surfer dudes!

It's a fact: Astronomers have found a diamond in the sky over Australia. A white dwarf star has been located with a 1,864-mile-wide core of crystallized carbon, or diamond. It weighs 10 billion trillion trillion carats.

WHAT IN THE WORLD?

Citric Scene

Feast your eyes on this mouthwatering model of the Taj Mahal Palace in India. Made entirely of oranges and lemons, and weighing 140 tons, it was created in February 2007 for the 74th annual Lemon Festival in Menton, France. The real Taj Mahal is made of totally inedible white marble.

Close to the Bone

A floating stage on Lake Constance in Bregenz, Austria, made a big splash with audiences at Verdi's opera *A Masked Ball*. In July 1999, lakeside operagoers sat openmouthed as a grizzly skeleton stared spookily down at the giant, open-book theater. One "page" formed the spectacular stage, the other made up the backdrop.

Made in China

Hundreds of porcelain plates, spoons, and bowls were the building blocks for an eight-foot-high elephant in February 2007, at the Xinjiang Uygur Spring Festival, in northwestern China. Not just a pretty face, the elephant was illuminated by lightbulbs and became a giant-sized lamp. Other light-fantastic designs at the festival included a 328-foot-long dragon.

Paper Craft

After toying with milk cartons over breakfast, artist Frank Bölter took just two hours to fold Tetrapack paper—which is what cartons are often made from—and make it shipshape. He launched his life-size paper boat in August 2007 onto the River Elbe, at Laurenburg, Germany. The bottom of the 30-foot, 55-pound boat got soggy, but Frank calculated it would float for 40 days.

It's a fact: The giant rocking stone of Mount Cimino, Italy, is 28 feet long and weighs 385 tons, yet it rocks to and fro on its base without falling over.

ATTENTION SEEKERS

Pulling Strings

Architects in Huainan, southeast China, have been instrumental in constructing a building on a distinctly musical note. Visitors to the amazing structure built in October 2007 enter through a violin and go upstairs to the first floor into a grand piano. It's thought to be a way of encouraging the town's children to learn to play the two instruments.

Save Driving

A sports manufacturer scored with motorists during the Soccer World Cup in Germany in May 2006 with a 213-foot-long billboard of German goalkeeper Oliver Kahn, who stretched over four lanes of traffic on the way to Munich Airport.

Advertising Space

Dale Gardner, an astronaut on the Space Shuttle *Discovery*, held up the world's most remote "For Sale" sign in November 1984 during a space walk. Supposedly going to the highest bidder were two old satellites—but it was just a joke. More seriously, one well-known pizza company did pay for their 30-foot logo on an unmanned rocket, and there's been at least one proposal for a colossal billboard in low orbit—one that could be seen from Earth.

Melting Moment

Chocoholics were invited not just to gaze but to graze at a giant billboard in London, England, in April 2007. A chocolate company spent a month creating their 14½ x 9½ foot edible Easter display. Passersby couldn't wait to munch their way through the 10 bunnies, 72 eggs, and 128 panels. It was all gone in just three hours!

RIPLEY R REWARD

15

PLAYING BALL

Claws Encounter

Here's a new twist on getting up close and personal with dangerous beasts. In April 2007, at Stukenbrock Safari Park in Germany, performance artist Arnd Drossel rolled into the tiger enclosure inside a hand-built ball of steel wire. The beasts were baffled, but the wheel of steel, crafted from 250 wire strands, stood up to their big cat curiosity. Drossel was soon off again on his 13-mile-a-day hike across Germany, living, eating, and sleeping inside his rolling cage.

It's a Miracle

If you don't like swimming, why not try strolling—or even jogging—on water? With the aid of the walk-on-water ball, that's exactly what people are doing on Lake Xibei Wuhan, China. Inside big inflatable balloons, they can exercise and play on the water's surface without getting wet. The zipper lets in and out up to three people. They can then have a dry splash around for up to ten minutes—before the air runs out!

‹‹ Ripley Rewind ‹‹‹‹‹‹‹‹‹‹‹‹‹‹‹

A Mail Thing

Fred W. Miller of Newark, New Jersey, made this ball weighing 8½ pounds from 75,000 cancelled U.S. postage stamps.

endurance

IN A SPIN

In November 2006, the magician and endurance star David Blaine took "hanging out" to new limits when he was dangled a death-defying 50 feet above the ground. To make the stunt even more spectacular, he was spun inside a giant gyroscope for three days without food or water.

David Blaine was suspended from a crane above New York's famous Times Square.

The three steel rings were programmed to flip him up to eight times a minute. As if that wasn't enough, he was also chained in on the final day and given just 16 hours to escape his shackles. Being David Blaine, he managed magically to free himself in no time and raised money for the Salvation Army, which had clothed him when he was a child. As a result, 100 underprivileged children each received $500 to go on a shopping spree.

STREETWISE

Switchback Street

Wend your way down San Francisco's Lombard Street, and be ready to swerve—sharply. The steep descent is regarded as America's most crooked street. A series of eight zig-zags lined by a blaze of colorful flowers keeps drivers well within the speed limit of five miles per hour.

Fine Line

Be careful when parking in Highbury Crescent, London. You might miss the tiniest of "No Parking" yellow lines—only 18 inches long—and end up with a fine. It's so small that a car tire would barely cover it and many people think it's a waste of paint. However, local authorities say it's a way of separating residents' spaces from paid parking areas, and making sure drivers don't park in the wrong zone.

Shark-Fin Roof

New High Street in Headington, England, is lined with terraced houses. It's a normal scene, except for one jaw-dropping detail: the 25-foot-long great white shark plunging into the roof at No. 2. Bill Heine attached the fiberglass model created by John Buckley to his house in 1986.

Fire Starters

More than 20,000 people gathered in Great Torrington, England, in August 2000 to see London burning. It wasn't the actual city burning, but a full-size replica of Pudding Lane, where the Great Fire of London started in 1666. It took the Great Torrington Cavaliers—fund-raisers for charity—almost one year to plan and two years to build their reconstruction. The street, complete with bakery, jail, and church, was on display to the public for one month, then set ablaze. After just two hours, it was unrecognizable; by morning, only three inches of ash remained.

It's a fact: In November 2004, the entire 111-foot-high Fu Gang building in Wuzhou, China, was picked up and moved mechanically 116 feet over 11 days— the heaviest house removal in history.

Falling Meat

Imagine walking along the street to find lumps of meat falling from the sky! That's what happened over a small area of Bath County, Kentucky, in 1876. The meat turned out to be lung tissue, maybe from a horse, but experts rejected the idea that it had been disgorged by flying buzzards. No one ever figured out how it got there.

On the Ball

At a factory in Tewkesbury, England, in 1996, there was a light display—and it was all caused by ball lightning from a thunderstorm. A blue and white sphere of light the size of a tennis ball whizzed around inside the building, hitting machinery and sending sparks flying, before hitting a window and exploding with an orange flash and a terrific bang. Three people received electric shocks.

Cola Bomb

People in Keokuk, Iowa, were busy enjoying the July 4th celebrations in 1995 when they were suddenly hit by a shower of soft-drink cans! A huge tornado had swept the cans up into the air from a cola-bottling plant in Moberly and carried them 150 miles north before dropping them on Keokuk.

Shrimp Shower

In April 2005, on Mount Soledad, California, hundreds of tiny crustaceans fell from the sky during a storm. Scientists say shrimp tend to congregate in shallow water in bad weather and were probably carried inland by a tornado at sea.

Hail Horror

Hailstones more than twice the size of tennis balls fell over Aurora, Nebraska, during a 2003 storm. The biggest one measured 7 inches in diameter and had a circumference of 18¾ inches—and that was after a big chunk had broken off on impact and a bit more had melted!

Blood Rain

Rain can ruin your day, but when it's red and stains your clothes, it's even worse. Red rain fell sporadically over Kerala, India, for two months in 2001—and nobody knows why. Could it have been dust transported from the deserts of the Arabian Peninsula, blood from a flock of bats killed at high altitude, or red particles from a small comet that disintegrated entering the Earth's atmosphere?

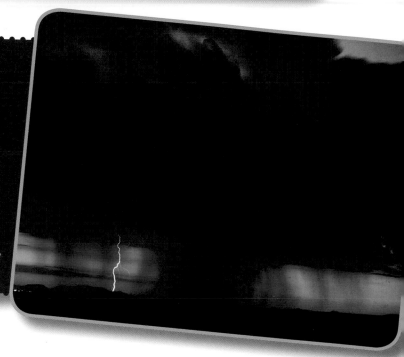

Human Hailstorm

How creepy is this? Five glider pilots, caught in a thundercloud over German mountains in 1930, bailed out, but were carried up and down within the super-cooled cloud. Finally they plummeted to earth, frozen within prisons of ice. Only one survived.

Web of Intrigue

Mysterious white spiderlike webs—some as big as 60 feet long—fell over Wisconsin in 1881. They seemed to float inland from Lake Michigan in thick sheets, stretching as far as the eye could see. Spookily, no spiders were reported in any of the webs.

It's a fact:

Ball lightning can sometimes pass through a glass window without breaking it. But other times—and nobody knows why—the glass is smashed to pieces.

SIZE PRIZE

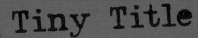

Tiny Title

The pages of this book are so tiny that the book can lie open and still be no bigger than the length of the eye of a needle! In December 2000, Taiwanese artist Chen Frong-shean presented his 155-word, 14-page version of *Little Polar Bear*. At 0.031 x 0.035 inches, it's the smallest book ever, tinier than his *Little Prince*, which balances on the tip of a ballpoint pen.

Long on the Draw

In November 2006, pupils at Nicolae Tonitza High School in Bucharest, Romania, put down their paintbrushes. They had completed the longest painting made by children. It measured 11,365 feet. The kids spent six hours a day for two weeks painting flowers to create this super-stretched floral artwork.

Soccer to Me

If it isn't your style to wear a full soccer uniform to show support for your team, here's a more subtle way to demonstrate you're a fan. A turf-covered sneaker, complete with pint-sized players. Where's it been seen? In soccer-mad Barcelona, Spain, of course.

Midget Mares

In June 2003, three apparently very tiny horses were seen seeking shelter under some garden furniture in a field near Erfurt, Germany. It wasn't a trick of the camera, but a result of brilliantly crafted oversized items made by a local wood merchant, who had put the furniture out to pasture!

>> Ripley Rewind <<<<<<<<

Clean Sweeper

This broom, made in Deshler, Nebraska, could really sweep you away. Originally 13 feet across and 40 feet high, it was later made into 1,440 smaller brooms.

It's a fact: Minuscule alphabet soup was created at UCLA in 2007. Scientists use lasers to move the letters, which are ten times smaller than a human hair—showing they can work in tiny spaces, such as inside cells.

WHAT'S UP?

Cold Goal

One of the highest-altitude soccer matches to be played on an artificial field kicked off on June 8, 2007, at nearly 11,500 feet. The venue was the permanently snow- and ice-covered Jungfrau Glacier in the European Alps. It's so high that the thin air meant the match could last only ten minutes. The players in their skimpy shirts and shorts were promoting the ultimate European soccer championship—EURO 2008. Strangely, the exhibition match might have been banned under rules that state no soccer game should be played over 8,000 feet! The game ended in a dizzying 5–5 draw!

At His Peak

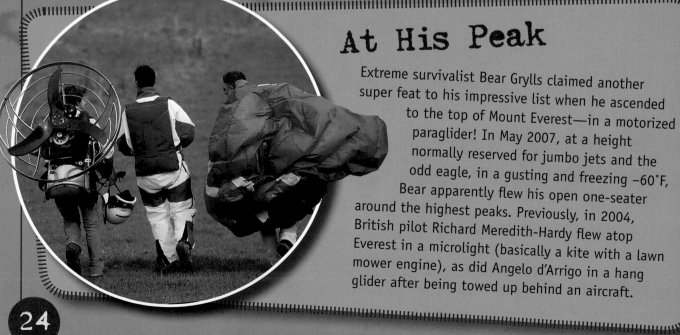

Extreme survivalist Bear Grylls claimed another super feat to his impressive list when he ascended to the top of Mount Everest—in a motorized paraglider! In May 2007, at a height normally reserved for jumbo jets and the odd eagle, in a gusting and freezing –60°F, Bear apparently flew his open one-seater around the highest peaks. Previously, in 2004, British pilot Richard Meredith-Hardy flew atop Everest in a microlight (basically a kite with a lawn mower engine), as did Angelo d'Arrigo in a hang glider after being towed up behind an aircraft.

TOP TABLE

The friends sat down to a four-course meal of **caviar**, smoked duck, and **chocolate** pudding, followed by a cheese selection.

The drinks were already chilled when six diners sat down for supper at a freezing −40°F. The view was awesome because they were seated at 22,000 feet, just 7,000 feet below the summit of the world's highest mountain, Everest. In May 2004, dressed in top hats and formal wear, the dining climbers carried their chairs and table up the slope along with a white tablecloth, plates, cutlery, wine glasses, and even a candelabra. It was all part of their bid to enjoy the world's highest formal dinner. Being environmentally conscious, they removed all uneaten food, the furniture, and other equipment. It's not the highest meal ever. In June 2005, Bear Grylls hosted the highest freestanding dinner party at a table suspended below a hot air balloon at 24,500 feet.

freezing

DIG IN!

Fancy a Lick?

Everyone loves a Popsicle, but one with a wriggly worm in it sounds gross. Not for Annie Munoz: In June 2007, she launched her collection of Popsicles filled with grasshoppers and oatmeal worms in Panama City. Annie reckons such tasty morsels will be a hit in Central America and China.

Bean Where?

Fancy a cup of Kopi Luwak? That's Indonesian for Civet Cat Coffee and it's the most expensive coffee in the world! The ripest coffee beans are eaten by the civet cats, who pass them semi-digested as pellets! These beans are then harvested from the forest floor, cleaned, and partially roasted to lock in the taste.

Lengthy Leek

In September 2002, five-year-old Abbey Yarde held aloft a high-rise leek. Grown by Fred Charlton from Easington, England, it weighed 17 pounds, 13 ounces.

Super-Size Fries

In February 2004, Alan Williams of Hereford, England, fried up more than 800 pounds of potatoes to produce a bag of French fries weighing over 400 pounds. An amazing 50 pounds of salt and 30 gallons of vinegar were also on hand to make the fries as tasty as possible. It worked. Not one fry went uneaten in this charity event.

It's a fact: In 1997, Harry Hurley of North Carolina grew a green bean that was 4 feet 4 inches long.

20

RIPLEY'S TRAVELS

20 In Jamaica, Ripley saw a tree with oysters growing on it. The oysters fasten themselves to the mangrove trees on the banks of saltwater lagoons.

1 Ripley received a letter written on the back of a Japanese stamp addressed only "Ripley—North America." It was mailed in Yokohama and was delivered to Ripley in New York City.

2 Ripley went to the village with one of the world's longest names, Llanfairpwllgwyngyllgog-erychwyrndrobwllllanty-siliogogogoch in Wales.

19 Ripley was in the Bahamas in 1940 when news came of two British seamen found unconscious on the shoreline. Their ship torpedoed, they had survived 70 days at sea in a rowboat.

18 On the island of St. Croix, Virgin Islands, Ripley held in his hand a fruit of the Poison Manchineel tree, thought to be the most poisonous tree in the world.

17 "Panama hats are made in Ecuador—not in Panama. They got the name simply because Panama used to be the great trading center where most of them were bought and sold," Ripley wrote.

16 "Water freezes every night of the year at Alto Crucero, in Bolivia, while at noon-day the sun is hot enough to blister the flesh," noted Ripley.

15 Ripley in Kenya, near Lake Magadi, stands beside a white driver ants' nest, constructed around a tree. Eventually the ants kill the tree and devour the wood.

14 On the River Nile banks, opposite Karnak's ruins, Ripley found a 64-foot statue that was reputed to speak. On the legs of the statue were 87 inscriptions quoting the day and time when people heard it, among them Emperor Hadrian, Tacitus, and Pliny.

13 In front of the Gate of the Citadel, Ripley saw the Chair of the Ages on which was written: "Only he who by the will of God has lived 100 years may sit here."

3

Ripley got stuck in snow on Russia's Georgian Military Highway. Aided by two oxen, they pushed the car up the pass.

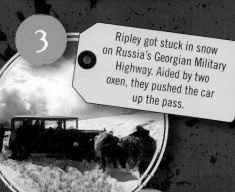

5

The Lighthouse Man, wrote Ripley in his travel journal, went about the streets of Chungking, China, with a lit red candle seven or eight inches in length stuck into his scalp. A hole had been made in his skull to hold the candle, which was held firm with sealing wax.

4

Fedor Machow of Charkow was a famous Russian giant who had a hand two feet long.

6

Ripley reported on elephant-shaped statuary at Nanking, China. Their presence suggests that elephants were known in early times in China.

7

The Great Rangoon Temple—Shwe Dagon Pagoda—was built to house three hairs from the head of Buddha. The Burmese believe that anyone coming within 1,000 miles of a single hair will be protected from evil.

8

9

For a wedding ring, Fijians wear the tooth of a sperm whale hung from a plaited coconut husk fiber.

Ripley encountered tribesmen of New Guinea, some of whom proudly displayed decorated trophy skulls from their headhunting raids.

12

On the streets of Calcutta, India, Ripley met fakirs, who performed acts of endurance as part of their religion. One man always walked on all fours.

11

Ripley visited Ayers Rock near Alice Springs, Australia—a massive stone outcropping in the desert. It stands 1,143 feet aboveground and sinks 1½ miles into the ground.

10

Ripley wrote, "There are pine trees in New Zealand with needles sometimes over two feet long. They do not grow exactly like an American pine. They look like snakes, but are very bristly."

The Last Word

29

That's Corny!

The renowned competitive eater, Crazy Legs Conti, was buried alive under 100 cubic feet of popcorn in "The Popcorn Sarcophagus." Breathing through a snorkel as he ate, he used colored lights to signal— red meant "danger," green meant "OK," and yellow meant "alert, need more butter!"

Chapter 2

FLAKY FOLK

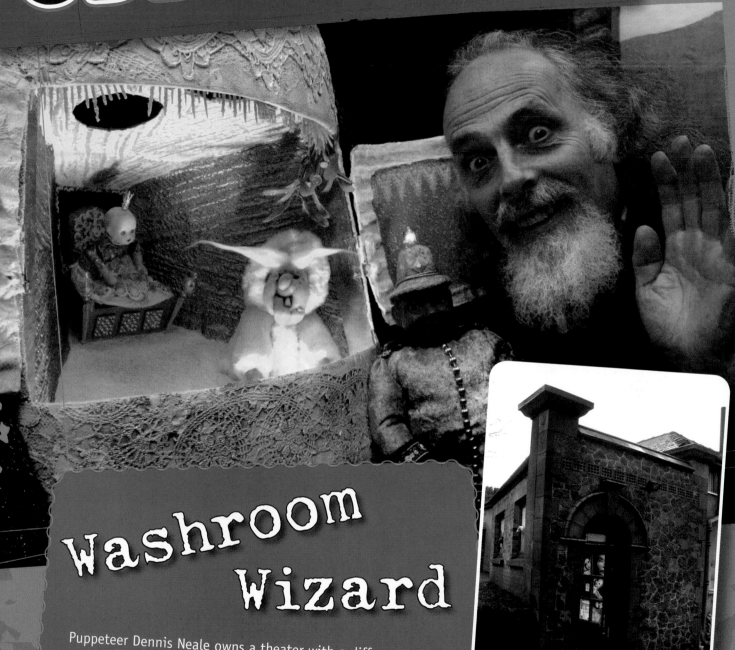

Washroom Wizard

Puppeteer Dennis Neale owns a theater with a difference—it was once a public restroom. In 1999, he converted the men's washroom into a stage, and the ladies' cubicles into 12 seats. His puppet shows and poetry readings are a sellout in the compact (16 x 9 x 6 feet) arts center in Worcestershire, England. Now that's convenient!

Sound Man

Ever imagine turning your backyard fence into a musical instrument? Henry Dagg of Kent, England, did just that. This musician, classically trained on the cello—and self-taught on the piano, bass guitar, and metal saw—spent five years and $100,000 building and fine-tuning his metal fence and gates to create a giant glockenspiel. In German, Glocke is "bell" and spiel means "play."

Park Life

Movie fan Andrew Simpson of York, England, loved the dinosaur epic *Jurassic Park* so much that he built his own backyard prehistoric theme park. The 17-year-old took two years to design his downsized dino park. Entering under the 13-foot "Jurassic" gateway, visitors could enjoy a mini-water ride and check out the life-size scientist and giant reptile models.

Festive Frolics

1 Every year in Manitou Springs, Colorado, teams build and race coffins with a living female occupant. They are replaying the legend of Emma Crawford, who was buried atop Red Mountain in 1890, only to have her coffin slide down the canyon in 1929 after heavy rains.

2 Brisbane, Australia, is the venue for the annual roach-racing world championships. Complete with bagpipers to open the show and race stewards to monitor the events, the cockroaches go to the races every year on Australia Day.

3 Each July 4, at Oatman, Arizona, contestants try to fry eggs using only the sun and some aluminum foil, magnifying glasses, or solar devices. The first to fry an egg in under 15 minutes wins. One even cooked potatoes and bacon with his egg.

It's a fact:
Once a year, grandfathers and grandsons get together in teams in Fort Worth, Texas, to race curled-up armadillos.

DANGER ZONE

Go With the Flow

Russian kids in the Amur Bay Arctic region like to leap over ice floes for fun. It's scary because the ice is thin and cracks in the spring. Sometimes the teenagers end up stranded on a tiny ice floe offshore, and have to be rescued. Possibly it's a pastime that should be left to the region's real masters of the ice-floe hop—polar bears.

Dirty Play

In July 2007, some 500 athletes got down and dirty in the slimy mudflats by the River Elbe. They were competing in possibly the world's dirtiest sporting event—the annual *Wattolympiade*, or mud-olympics, at Brunsbüttel, Germany. Soccer, handball, and a mud-eel race were among the events that took place in more than two feet of mud.

Chain Male

The jokes Nathan Zorchak tells while he's juggling may suggest he's not concentrating, but chances are he is. That's because he's throwing and catching three roaring chainsaws. Then he's on to juggling scythes and bowling balls.

Ripley Rewind

ANNIE EDSON TAYLOR
HEROINE OF NIAGARA FALLS
F. M. RUSSELL

Fall Girl

In 1901, Annie Edson Taylor was the first person to survive going over Niagara Falls in a barrel. She was in the barrel for 1 hour 15 minutes before being rescued.

OUTRAGEOUS!

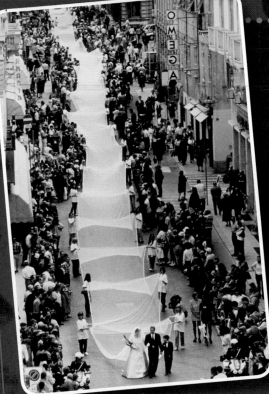

Bride Pride

Weddings are wonderful affairs with the bride in a beautiful flowing gown often topped off with a modest veil. There was nothing modest about Claudia Armillei's veil when she got married in May 1996. The 23-year-old's headdress flowed not just along the church aisle in Ascoli Piceno, Italy, but out into the street, leaving a trail measuring 1,320 feet. Some 50 helpers and passersby kept the train of lace, ribbon, and mesh fabric on track as the couple walked to their wedding ceremony.

Toupee-ed Tots

Most babies have little hair and it's sometimes embarrassing trying to guess if a baby you meet is a boy or girl. So a California-based firm came up with a hair-raising solution—baby wigs! Instead of a bonnet or woolly hat, why not order a dreadlock wig, a copper mop, or even cute pink curls?

IRON MAN

Every time Phil Shaw from Leicester, England, wanted to go rock climbing, he found he had stacks of ironing to get through. Phil, taking the name "Steam," climbed to the top of peaks with his board and then got busy with some outdoor ironing. This stunt, and others in the late 1990s, triggered the first world extreme ironing championships in the village of Valley near Munich, Germany. In September 2002, contestants from ten countries competed in combining an extreme sport with the art of clothes-smoothing using battery-powered irons.

One man ironed 60 feet underwater in scuba gear. Another competitor attempted ironing while surfing on a small river.

Judges looked for the best-pressed tea towels, T-shirts, and boxer shorts, as well as fantastic sporting skills.

smooth operator

THAT'S BRAVE

Toe Curling

Don't try this at home! In Nanjing Xuanjing Lake Park in China, in October 2005, a woman performed the ultimate in stunning stunts: standing barefoot on sharp knife blades and walking over switched-on lightbulbs. Mind-boggling!

Tear Jerker

A Chinese stuntman performed an amazing test of strength when he lifted two buckets of water using just his eyelids. The buckets, attached to ropes, were clipped onto his eyelids which can't have been pleasant even before the water was added. You've got to wonder if he could open his eyes afterwards.

Stand by Me

Indian yogis (meditation experts) are famous for feats of endurance. They can sleep on a bed of nails, or stay buried for long periods. In 1974, in Agra, India, a yogi used his amazing breathing control to literally bury his head in the sand. His breathing slowed down so much that his pulse was recorded at two beats per minute. A normal heart rate is anywhere between 60 and 100 beats per minute.

Raising the Roof

In August 2006, three plucky cello players clambered 330 feet up stone stairs, avoided the pigeon droppings, and performed on the rooftop of Liverpool Cathedral, England. They were completing a 12-day charity drive of rooftop-playing at all 42 Anglican cathedrals in England. They wanted to raise $10,000 for good causes.

It's a fact: For 12.22 seconds in November 2005, Zafar Gill, from Pakistan, lifted 121 pounds—suspended from one of his ears!

HOT WHEELS

POWER WAGON

Dazzling Driver

Sheikh Hamad Bin Hamdan Al Nahyan, from the United Arab Emirates, has collected some awesome automobiles. His trio of power wagon trucks—giant, standard, and minuscule—are all driveable, and the big one is home to bedrooms, bathrooms, and a kitchen. It would even have stood out at the world's largest truck convoy in September 2007, when 1,800 trucks snaked their way along North American freeways. The sheikh also owns the world's largest trailer home—an earth-painted sphere with eight bedrooms and nine bathrooms.

And Stretch

Known as "The King of Show Cars," Jay Ohrberg builds celebrity movie and TV cars. His creations include the vehicles in *Batman Returns*, as well as the Flintstones' cars. This is his pink Cadillac guitar-car. It's not his longest—that honor goes to a 120-foot Cadillac with a swimming pool on board.

Bell Boy

Cycle maker Didi Senft cast 10,000 bicycle bells into the shape of a fish to make his *klingelfisch* ("bell fish" in German) bicycle. He then rode it in Strokow (near Berlin) in March 2007. Didi has built more than 100 cycling contraptions, including the biggest rideable two-wheeler ever, which stands at 25½ feet long and 12 feet high.

Bat-mobile

In March 2007, Sudhakar Yadav steered his 25-foot-long cricket-bat-shaped car in the Indian city of Hyderabad. He was supporting the Indian team in the Cricket World Cup. "It can travel at forty miles per hour," he boasted.

It's a fact: Richard Moriarty of Newport Beach, California, has a Lamborghini sports car hanging from the wall of his house—as a piece of art!

SMART ART

Driven Crazy

Some show people can fill a theater with 1,000 people every night. And then there was Benji Ming, who couldn't fill his comic show with more than three people each night. So Benji hit on the new idea of inviting a ticket-buying audience of just one person to drive around with him at the Edinburgh Fringe Festival. His stage was an ultra-compact two-seater car in which he performed his three, ten-minute shows. Each new spectator sat next to Benji, while he taxied them about and told them his jokes.

Bathing Beauty

In November 2003, Mark McGowan settled himself into a nice, relaxing bath of baked beans. Just to complete the scene, he stuck two fries up his nostrils and strapped sausages to his head! He had his bath in an art gallery window, and after 100 hours Mark felt he had made his point, which was to protest against criticism by health experts of the Great British breakfast: a traditional meal of bacon, eggs, sausages, tomatoes, French fries, and fried bread. Some of his other demonstrations have involved pushing a peanut with his nose for seven miles, attaching his arm to a London lamppost for two weeks, and walking 11 miles backwards with a 27-pound raw turkey on his head.

HEAD BANGER

When some members of The Daredevil Opera Company's audience are wearing waterproof windbreakers, it's clear the show is unusual. You may not hear much opera in the performances, but there are plenty of "whiz-bangs," firebombs, and explosions from this part-circus, part-acrobatic, song-and-dance group. As well as performing death-defying stunts—fully throttled, razor-tooth chainsaws are juggled 44 times, and a running lawnmower is lifted aloft with someone's teeth—the company demonstrates an exploding head trick. Performer Colt Sandberg wears a military-style helmet with a watermelon perched on top of it. Did you know that blowing up red-fleshed melons is a trick used in movie special effects to mimic the gory and gooey moments of real-life explosions?

Colt's wacky idea was to make it look as if his head really exploded.

Happily, Colt's perfected the art and, unlike the watermelon, he survives every time. But he's not saying how he does it.

WHAT'S THEIR GAME?

Fire Ball

Pelota is one of the world's oldest ball games—it was played 3,400 years ago. In October 2005, to celebrate this ancient sport, a museum in Mexico City put on a match in which the players propelled a flaming rubber ball with hockey-style sticks.

Check Mate

Chess is a tricky game, requiring ice-cool nerve. British and Russian chessmasters took that literally when they competed on 70-square-yard chessboards in January 2007. The pieces, carved from ice, were prone to melting, so each player had just 30 seconds to make his move. They played via live satellite in London and Moscow.

Sweet-toothed Scramble

At midnight on May 25, 2007, climbers raced up a 60-foot tower covered in mock sweet buns on Hong Kong's Cheung Chau Island. Whoever bagged the most "lucky" buns was the winner. This bun scramble dates back 200 years when islanders sought to protect their fishermen against storms and the spirits of pirates.

Mega Moves

A giant-sized Scrabble® board, which virtually covered the soccer field of the old Wembley Stadium in London, was created in October 1998. The letters were the size of dining tables!

Scientists in Boston have proved that however jumbled up it may be, a Rubik's Cube can be solved in 26 twists or less. So get busy!

War Shrine

Each year at the Mitama Festival in Tokyo, Japan, around 30,000 paper lanterns are lit at a shrine to people who died in World War II. The four-day festival was started in 1947 at the city's Yasukuni Shrine to honor the two and a half million Japanese war dead. As many as 300,000 people turn up to see the poignant light display.

Died 100 Times

Stricken by a mystery virus, Jim McClatchey of Atlanta, Georgia, died 100 times in one day—but still survived! Admitted to the hospital, he suffered a series of cardiac arrests requiring emergency shock treatment, his heart stopping 50 times in the first hour alone. In fact, he had to be shocked back to life so frequently that he sustained second-degree burns to his chest. Miraculously, he was back to work not long after.

Dead Ringer

Thanks to a new invention, you can now talk to the dead! A German man, Jüergen Bröther, has devised the Phone Angel, consisting of a cell phone, powerful batteries, and a small loudspeaker, all housed in a waterproof container that can be buried next to a coffin. He wanted to speak to his late mother.

Buried Alive

In a new extreme sport, you can be buried five feet underground in a coffin for an hour! The coffin is linked by webcam so that friends and family can watch. It also has an oxygen supply and a panic button, and the sport's inventor, Dutch entertainer Eddy Daams, insists that it is perfectly safe.

Final Journey

Harold Saber really didn't want to trouble anyone. After suffering a heart attack in 2002, he drove himself to a New Jersey funeral home and died moments later in the parking lot. He had paid for his funeral ten years previously and had always vowed that he would make his own way to the home.

Funeral Fans

Most people go to a funeral to pay respects to the deceased, but an elderly New Zealand couple went for a different reason. They attended funerals of complete strangers five times a week for 20 years so they could enjoy the free food and drink!

Coffin Parade

If you're too tired to walk to church, get your family to carry you in a coffin. That's what they do in Ribarteme, Spain, for the annual Procession of the Shrouds. People who have cheated death during the year are carried in coffins to the church by family members, and then paraded through town to thank God for keeping them alive.

Ice Maiden

In 1993 a team of Russian archaeologists made an amazing discovery high in the Altai Mountains near the Mongolian border—a 2,500-year-old tomb containing the bodies of six horses, and a woman preserved in a block of ice in her coffin.

It's a fact: Jose Gomez of Ilhavo, Portugal, built a wooden replica of his Mercedes 220 CDI car. He plans to be buried in it.

FOOD FOR THOUGHT

Hot Dog Hero

Joey Chestnut of San Jose, California, must love his hot dogs. In July 2007 he wolfed down 66—buns and all—in just 12 minutes. That was enough to win the Nathan's 2007 International Hot Dog Eating Contest in Brooklyn, New York. Joey beat six-time champion Takeru Kobayashi by just three hot dogs!

Head Chefs

A food cart displaying human heads surrounded by various vegetables is not an enticing prospect. Thankfully, the human platter on show at the annual Carnival of Rijeka in Croatia in February 2007 was a clever illusion. It was part of the festive floats procession designed to scare off ancient evil spirits.

Metal Menu

French entertainer Michel Lotito from Grenoble is nicknamed *Monsieur Mangetout* ("Mr Eat-It-All"), because that's what he does. The 58-year-old eats bicycles, televisions, and even light aircraft with no ill effects. He has to take them apart and slurp down mineral oil before swallowing the smaller bits, but it's still a full-metal meal.

Worm Squirm

How many worms could you eat? In the fall of 2003, at Gatlinburg, Tennessee, survivalist Mark Hogg was buried up to his neck in a six-foot container crammed with 10,000 worms wriggling right up to his chin. His arms trapped, this ex-soldier from Louisville, Kentucky, slurped worms spaghetti-style for a whole hour.

Ripley Rewind

Slippery Tale

G.L Crooks of Baltimore, Maryland, ate 325 oysters at one three-hour sitting. Presumably, it was towards the start of his epic meal that this photograph of him looking fresh-faced was taken.

It's a fact: 80-year-old Yoshiro Nakamatsu has photographed and analyzed every meal he's eaten for 34 years. He wants to produce a nutrition powder with the essential ingredients to help you live for more than 140 years!

HISTORY HORROR

1 A ghoulish countess called Elizabeth Bathory (1560–1614) was accused of bathing in the blood of her female victims in her castle in Hungary. It was claimed her need for blood was to make herself more beautiful. Her modern nickname is Countess Dracula.

2 In 1962, the schools in Tanganyika, East Africa, had to be closed because of an outbreak of contagious laughter that lasted for six months!

4 The first known British actor to play on Broadway was George Frederick Cook in 1796. His remains are rumored to have later starred as Yorick, the jester whose skull appears in *Hamlet*.

3 In 1912, while campaigning for a third term as president, Theodore Roosevelt was shot in the chest by John Shrank. The force of the bullet was blunted by the wad of speech papers in his breast pocket. Although wounded, Roosevelt went on to finish his 90-minute speech.

20 A death curse was put on U.S. presidents by Shawnee Chief Tecumseh in 1811. He warned that presidents elected in years ending with a zero would die in office. But the curse seemed to end when Reagan survived being shot in 1981.

19 Spartan boys were trained to be tough. One story has it that a boy stole a live fox to kill and eat. When soldiers approached, the boy had to hide the fox beneath his cloak. He allowed the fox to gnaw him—without showing pain—rather than let the theft be revealed.

18 The Black Death, a contagious plague in fourteenth-century England, forced doctors to wear a strange bio-protective suit with a large birdlike beak head-piece. The beak was filled with vinegar and oils to mask the smell of dead and dying plague victims.

17 In 1597, Edward VI of England became king when he was only nine years old. He still went to school and often misbehaved. Since it was illegal to punish him, Edward had a slave, Barnaby Fitzpatrick, who was whipped on his behalf whenever he stepped out of line.

16 Emperor Gaius Caligula of Rome was sensitive about his hair. After he went bald as a young man, he made it a crime for anyone to look down from a high place as he passed. Caligula did however have lots of body hair, which he was equally sensitive about, and banned the talk of "hairy goats" in his presence!

15 Queen Juana (1479–1555) of Castile, Spain, was known as "Joan the Mad." When her husband, Philip the Handsome of Austria, died she opened his coffin every evening to hug him.

5 John "Half Hanged" Smith was so nicknamed because in 1705, while being hanged for burglary at Tyburn Tree, England, he received an unexpected pardon. He'd been hanging for about 15 minutes before he was cut down. Unbelievably, he recovered.

6 Couples tended to marry in June in medieval times because they still smelled good after their once-a-year bath in May! To hide any lingering body odor, brides would carry a bouquet of flowers. This started the custom of carrying a bouquet at weddings.

7 Niagara Falls experienced a break of half an hour in 1848, when an ice jam blocked the source river.

8 In the sixteenth century, the Bishop of Rochester, England, made the mistake of upsetting his chef. Seeing an opportunity to take revenge, the cook put a special herb in the bishop's food to give him and his guests diarrhea. Unfortunately, two guests died as a result, and King Henry VIII sentenced the chef to be boiled to death.

9 Up until the end of the 1900s, barbers not only cut hair, but also performed dentistry, set broken bones, and performed minor operations. The familiar red-striped barber-shop pole was originally designed for the customer to grip while the barber did his medical work!

10 The Ming Emperor Hung Wu (1368–1398) is known as the cruelest leader in the entire history of China. He killed so many people that government officials would say their last goodbyes to their families in the morning, and if they survived the day, would congratulate each other in the evening.

11 Archduke Francis Ferdinand of Austria hated having creases in his clothes, so for important occasions he insisted on being sewn into his robes. Unfortunately, on June 28, 1914, he was shot by an assassin and it was impossible to open any of his buttons to provide life-saving assistance. He bled to death.

12 President William Howard Taft (1909–1913) weighed a huge 350 pounds and once got stuck in his bathtub in the White House! They decided to make a special tub for him. It was so big that four normal-sized men could fit inside.

13 The Chinook tribe, from the Pacific Northwest of the U.S., valued having a flat skull so highly that they strapped their children between two boards, from head to toe, for the first year of their life to ensure a flat head.

14 In 1574, King Henry III of France visited Venice. The Italians covered the whole of St. Mark's Square with an awning painted with a starry sky, and covered the floor with elaborate oriental rugs.

Ballboy!

Not content with just playing with tennis balls, Auggie the dog learned some new tricks. His owner, Lauren Miller, was very proud of his ability to pick up five tennis balls in his mouth at the same time!

Chapter 3
ANIMAL ANTICS

MORE IS MORE

Looking Sheepish

Bump into this lamb and you'll certainly see double! He really does have two heads and was born on a farm in Gansu province, China, in June 2005. The lamb is in perfectly good health and can drink milk from either mouth.

It's a fact: There is a rare breed of dog in the Amazon basin that has two noses. The double-nosed Andean tiger hound is a hunting dog valued for its keen sense of smell.

Twice as Nice

"He loves all the attention he's been getting," said farm owner Nicky Janaway in February 2007, about her newfound friend. Stumpy was born with two extra legs behind the ones ducks normally waddle on. Nicky is looking after her cute, four-legged friend at Warrawee Duck Farm in Hampshire, England.

This Little Piggy

Farmyard animals usually have familiar faces, but that's not the case for those belonging to farmer Ke Kuaile. In March 2007, he had a special little pig born on his farm in Xi'an, China. It had two mouths, two snouts, and three eyes! Since this unique animal required special care, it was given to a wildlife park.

<< Ripley Rewind <<<<<<<<<<<<

Plucky Pony

Missing its front legs when it was born, this pony, owned by L. St. Greathouse in Cambria, Iowa, walked upright.

ALL CREATURES GREAT AND SMALL

Horsin' Around

Meet Thumbelina, a mere 17 inches above the ground. Even miniature horses usually reach 34 inches in height, so Thumbelina, born in St. Louis, Missouri, in 2001, is really unusual. There are 62½ inches between her and the withers of the tallest horse around, Radar, a Belgian cart horse from Texas.

Hefty Hopper

She may look like a giant cuddly toy, but Crystal is a real rabbit. Weighing in at a massive 27 pounds, Crystal was named the biggest rabbit in the world in 2003. Chelsea Nicholson (pictured here) looks after her for owner Sue Dooley who works at the Giant Rabbit Rescue Centre in Kemseley Britain, where Crystal lives.

Colossal Catch

Something rare showed up in the nets of the *San Aspiring* in February 2007. A massive, 33-foot, 990-pound squid was fished out of the Ross Sea, near Antarctica. It was the first intact male colossal squid ever seen. The fishermen were able to preserve the specimen for scientists to examine.

Little Lizard

At just over an inch long, the Pygmy Leaf Chameleon is one of the world's tiniest reptiles. There are 26 types of pygmy, or dwarf, chameleons living on leafy forest floors in Madagascar and Malawi, Africa. Like their larger cousins they can change their coat color to hide from predators.

It's a fact:

In Harbin, China, a small hen laid an egg weighing 6.7 ounces, which is three times bigger than a normal one.

FUN TIME!

Wacky Wigs

Wigmaker Ruth Regina has created the ultimate finishing touch for that complete canine wardrobe—designer dog hairpieces. In August 2006, she launched her doggie "rugs" from her wig store in Bay Harbor Islands, Florida. Made from synthetic or human hair, they can be dyed, highlighted, and styled to the owner's tastes. The store next door sells coats, tiaras, and visors for lapdogs, so why not wigs? Says Ruth, "Dogs are just little people in fur coats."

Pampered Pooch

The latest perk for that precious pet is a trip to the spa. Doted-on dogs can enjoy *pawzicures* and poochie makeovers. On a serious note, dogs do get arthritis and other ailments, just like humans. So it seems natural that pooches in pain might also benefit from long-practiced Eastern healing therapies. In Tokyo, Japan, dogs can try out a Dead Sea mudpack, which is great for skin complaints, and in Bangkok, Thailand, animal doctors lay heated stones over dogs' tired muscles and bones to relieve aches and pains.

GONE CAMPING

Thinking of the Doggie Day Camp gets our four-legged friends all worked up. As many as 25 dogs can jump on to their own colorful bus for the 19-mile trip to Cajic from downtown Bogotá, the capital of Colombia. Here the animals are encouraged to enjoy athletic events such as soccer and doggie paddle races. A doggie treadmill running machine tires them out and helps them fight the flab!

Dogs are given obedience training and **weight-loss** classes.

Everyone wins: pet owners seeking a break from daily dogwalking and poop-scooping in the big city get a dog-free day, and the dogs have fun. But sometimes the dogs are a bit too tired to tell their owners all about it when they get back home!

bow wow

WILDLIFE

A Nose for It

Elephants are among only a few animals who can recognize their reflection, so it's no surprise that they are clever enough to paint, here at Mae Sa elephant camp in Thailand. In 2000, elephant paintings, sold at Christie's in New York, raised a massive $50,000.

Some Bottle!

Maybe in the ocean he was used to opening bottles to get to messages, because after being found on a beach in January 2007, Octi the octopus (who now lives in the National Aquarium of New Zealand, in Napier), has no problem using his tentacles to twist off bottle tops to reach food inside.

Poodle Power

Introducing Pluto, a poodle seen crossing a street in Mie Prefecture, Japan, in June 2005. Don't think that this was a one-time moment. Pluto can stroll for up to ¾ mile on his hind legs.

Gooooooal!

Who knows if anyone explained the offside rule to them, but pallet surgeonfish played ball at the Sea Paradise aquarium in Hakkeijima, near Tokyo, during the 2006 Soccer World Cup. Naturally sporting the colors of Japan's national squad, the "Blue Samurai," these fish lose their color when stressed. Let's hope they never had to take penalties.

It's a fact: Jackson the terrier came within one vote of being appointed chairman of Congresbury Footpaths Group, England. Members argued that he'd attended more walks and club events than the winner.

RIPLEY
R
REWARD

Bad-Hair Life

Whipper the budgie is a rare bird indeed—an incredible genetic condition makes her feathers fluff out like a feather duster. Her parents kicked her out of their cage, but happily, owner Julie Hayward hand-reared the little fluffball in her New Zealand aviary. Whipper has become a star attraction for fans of her cute curls.

Fowl Play

Here's a story to ruffle any bird's feathers—assuming they have them. In May 2002, Israeli scientist Avigdor Cahaner revealed the first genetically modified naked chicken. He expects his feather-free version will speed up chicken production because farmers won't need to pluck them. The "walking roast chicken" has upset animal rights supporters.

Hideous Hound

Playfully named Yoda or ET by some, Elwood scooped the World's Ugliest Dog Contest in 2007 at the Sonoma-Marin Fair, California. A winsome Chinese Crested and Chihuahua mix weighing just six pounds, Elwood came second runner up in 2006, returning to triumph the following year. His Mohawk, goggly eyes, and wagging tongue were just too irresistible.

Puss in the Pink

Philip and Joan Worth were amazed when, on September 3, 2005, their snow-white feline came back from his daily catwalk all pretty in pink. How nine-year-old Brumas from Devon, England, acquired his "Barbie pink" fur remains a mystery. As for Brumas, he remains unruffled and unharmed.

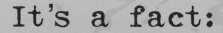

It's a fact: An American dentist has given his Persian cat gold teeth. David Steele of Alexandria, Indiana, fixed gold crowns, worth $1,900, on Sebastian's two protruding bottom canines to stop them breaking off.

CRAZY CRITTERS

Dolphin Dialect

Did you know that dolphins have regional accents? Scientists say that dolphins living off the coast of Wales have developed a different whistle from others around Britain. University experts are now trying to compile a dolphin dictionary to discover what the different sounds mean.

Bunny Hop

A reckless rabbit hitched a ride for 60 miles in the engine of a car in England in 2006. The rabbit was finally spotted peeking through the front air grille of the Ford Mondeo, and the engine had to be partly dismantled so that the furry stowaway could be rescued.

Crafty Cat

When a small bird in Brazil hurt itself falling out of its nest in 2006, it might have expected to be eaten by a passing cat. However, the cat had other ideas and decided to adopt it. The pair ate meat from the same plate and the cunning cat even used its feathered friend to help catch other birds!

Digitally Enhanced

A cat in Wales has 26 toes—that's eight more than normal cats. Whereas cats usually have five toes on each front paw and four on each hind paw, Alison Thomas of Swansea reports that her cat, Des, has seven toes on his front paws and six on the back.

When Gary Rosheisen of Columbus, Ohio, fell from his wheelchair in 2005, his pet cat called 911! Rosheisen had previously tried to teach Tommy to call 911, and it seems the training worked, as the cat managed to hit all the right buttons. Obviously Tommy couldn't explain what was wrong on the phone, but the silence alerted the police.

Doh! Nuts

A dog that loves donuts was blamed for starting a house fire in New Hampshire, in 2006 that caused $75,000 worth of damage. Investigators think the hungry hound jumped up to reach a box of donuts and accidentally switched on the stove.

Wobbly Pelicans

Four pelicans were rounded up in Los Angeles in June 2006—because they were drunk! One California Brown pelican hit a car windshield and the other three were found wandering dazed in the streets. Experts think the birds may have eaten fermented algae in the ocean.

Baby Boom

One mother shark had a lot of mouths to feed. Caught in May 2006, near Boca Grande, Florida, the 14½-foot-long female hammerhead shark was found to be pregnant with 55 babies—that's twice as many as usual!

It's a fact:

A porcupine can swallow large quantities of prussic acid without coming to any harm, although the same amount of acid would be enough to poison 100 humans.

CROSSING CULTURES

In a Mix

What do you get if you cross a horse with a zebra? A zorse of course! In August 2003, N'Soko, photographed here with his mom and dad, became the second zorse to be born in an animal park in Cucery, France—a world first. Can you guess the mixes behind yattles, ligers, and camas?

Nitted Together

They may not be the most obvious of soul mates, but these two cuddling creatures are the best of friends. Pluk, a four-year-old monkey, hugs and checks one-year-old Pom for lice at a temple in the Thai city of Ayutthaya, in August 2002. Both animals were abandoned by their owners at the temple a year prior. They have been inseparable ever since.

Claws for Thought

When a circus tiger abandoned her two newborn cubs, an unlikely four-legged nurse came to the rescue. In January 2007, Lilica the dog settled down to feed the tiger cubs from Casca, Brazil. Lilica has now joined the circus to be with the cubs.

<< Ripley Rewind <<<<<<<<<

Pig News

Is it a calf, or is it a pig? This strange creature was owned by Franks Sanville of Lebanon, New Hampshire.

MY FAMILY AND OTHER ANIMALS

Posing Pooches

Dog lovers across the globe are discovering they can involve their four-legged friends in many aspects of their lives. In February 2007, Satoe Tachi and her Kaninchen Dachshund, Chaco, enrolled for canine yoga, or "doga," lessons. It was organized by the Japan Dog Yoga Association to benefit both dog and owner, with traditional yoga breathing exercises and stretching poses. One stretch is even called the "downward-facing dog."

Hyenas at Home

If you found having a pet hamster or a fish a bit boring, maybe taking on a dog or cat would be the next step. Not so in the Shwaykani household, in Garamana, Syria, where there's a pet hyena or two. Hyenas have some of the strongest jaws in the animal kingdom, so they wouldn't be everyone's pet choice. Faten Shwaykani and her son Noureddin bathe the hyenas in the family bathroom, feed them eggs at the breakfast table, and let them lounge around at home. Everyone's kept all their fingers and toes—so far.

68

ROAMING THE HOME

Jim and Linda Sautner from Alberta, Canada, are proud owners of possibly the heaviest house pet in the world.

By April 2004, Bailey the buffalo weighed in at a staggering 1,600 pounds.

Leaving hoof marks on the carpet doesn't seem to upset his owners. In fact Bailey has been coming in, watching TV with the family, and generally making himself at home since 2000. At meal times, Bailey is called to the kitchen table and eats from his own bowl while Jim has coffee. Jim has a buffalo-meat business, but Bailey, the much-pampered pet, is not destined for the butcher's block. The other good news is that the U.S. bison population, which was once down to 1,000 because of mass killings in the late 1800s, is now up to 350,000.

massive

WORKING IT!

Tob-hog-an

Horse-drawn sleighs in a winter wonderland make a heartwarming Christmas image, but sleds pulled by snow-plowing pigs are more unusual. Heavyweight 1,000-pound potbellied pigs provided the hogpower to carry passengers at the Xiedao ski resort near Beijing, China, in December 2004.

It's a fact: The owner of a potbellied pig said she needed the pig as a therapeutic companion on a U.S. Airways flight in 2000. During the flight, Charlotte the pig entered the cockpit, refusing to leave until bribed with food.

Pick-up Pooch

Yelling "Go fetch!" starts many a dog scurrying after a stick. For faithful pooch Hei Zi, it's the command for a more sedate stroll round the block to pick up the groceries. Zi's owner, in Xianglan, China, has trained his dog to go shopping at the local market, using a specially designed saddle to carry his purchases.

Oh No, Overdrawn Again!

Cash withdrawal at ATM machines is a convenience for people. But now it seems some dogs are getting into the act. Canine Partners in Midhurst, England, have trained dogs to assist disabled owners in all walks of life, including taking out money from the bank.

<< Ripley Rewind <<<<<<<<<

Playing Ball

Rather than lugging his golf clubs around 18 holes, William Beck trained his Labrador to act as his golf caddy.

20

TAKE A GUESS

See page 143 for the answers!

1 Which is the only animal that can't jump?
A. Rhinoceros B. Elephant
C. Hog D. Chameleon

2 How many noses does a slug have?
A. 7 B. 1 C. 4 D. 3

3 What doesn't a starfish have?
A. A heart B. A brain
C. Eyes D. All of the above

20 Which animal's brain is smaller than its eye?
A. Ostrich B. Wombat
C. Toad D. Camel

19 Which is the most poisonous fish in the world?
A. Pufferfish B. Stonefish
C. Piranha D. Stingray

14 A poison-arrow frog has enough poison in its body to kill how many people?
A. 15 B. 200 C. 500 D. 2,200

18 What fish has over 350 light organs on its body?
A. Viperfish B. Starfish
C. Parrotfish D. Stingray

15 What is the strength of an electric eel's shock?
A. 400 volts B. 250 volts
C. 100 volts D. 500 volts

17 Which insect has the shortest life span?
A. Bee B. Common fly
C. Ant D. Moth

16 Pound for pound, which is the strongest animal in the world?
A. Elephant B. Hippopotamus
C. Rhinoceros D. Rhinoceros beetle

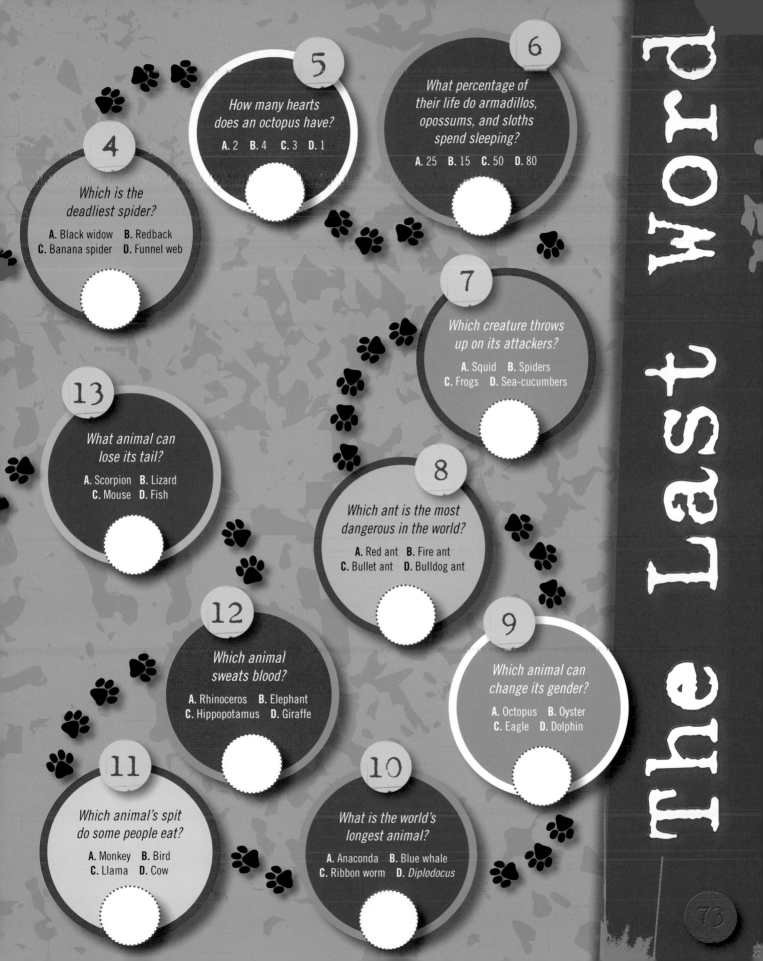

5 How many hearts does an octopus have?

A. 2 **B.** 4 **C.** 3 **D.** 1

6 What percentage of their life do armadillos, opossums, and sloths spend sleeping?

A. 25 **B.** 15 **C.** 50 **D.** 80

4 Which is the deadliest spider?

A. Black widow **B.** Redback
C. Banana spider **D.** Funnel web

7 Which creature throws up on its attackers?

A. Squid **B.** Spiders
C. Frogs **D.** Sea-cucumbers

13 What animal can lose its tail?

A. Scorpion **B.** Lizard
C. Mouse **D.** Fish

8 Which ant is the most dangerous in the world?

A. Red ant **B.** Fire ant
C. Bullet ant **D.** Bulldog ant

12 Which animal sweats blood?

A. Rhinoceros **B.** Elephant
C. Hippopotamus **D.** Giraffe

9 Which animal can change its gender?

A. Octopus **B.** Oyster
C. Eagle **D.** Dolphin

11 Which animal's spit do some people eat?

A. Monkey **B.** Bird
C. Llama **D.** Cow

10 What is the world's longest animal?

A. Anaconda **B.** Blue whale
C. Ribbon worm **D.** *Diplodocus*

Set in Concrete!

Canadian escape artist Dean Gunnarson freed himself from a locked box filled with two tons of wet cement. Gunnarson was chained and padlocked around his whole body and bound with several pairs of handcuffs. He managed to get out in only 2 minutes 43 seconds!

Chapter 4
AGAINST THE ODDS

BE A SPORT

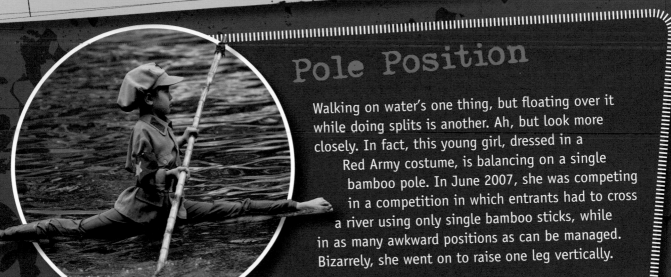

Pole Position

Walking on water's one thing, but floating over it while doing splits is another. Ah, but look more closely. In fact, this young girl, dressed in a Red Army costume, is balancing on a single bamboo pole. In June 2007, she was competing in a competition in which entrants had to cross a river using only single bamboo sticks, while in as many awkward positions as can be managed. Bizarrely, she went on to raise one leg vertically.

For the High Jump

How high can you pogo? How about leaping five feet using a gravity-defying pogo. Push down on the shaft and 12 rubber thrusters inside create massive spring-like tension. When the rider pulls up—*boingggg*—the thrusters release up to 1,200 pounds of thrust, creating a bounce higher than any pogo has gone before.

Board Out of His Mind

Lying on a four-foot-long skateboard with a kerosene-fuelled engine at the back, Joel King from Woodbridge, England, set a new luge world land-speed record of 110 miles per hour in August 2007. Lying with his head just two inches from the jet engine didn't seem to worry him; the cross wind did—the board had absolutely no mechanism for steering.

Red Sleds

RIPLEY
R
REWARD

The engine roared and growled, and Canadian freestyle "Sledneck" Lee Stuart skiied down the ramp. His 550-pound snowmobile shot 50 feet into orbit beside Moscow's famous onion-shaped domes! It was November 2005, and 35,000 spectators gasped in awe as Russia's historic Red Square, dominated by St. Basil's Cathedral, became the coolest motor sport venue ever.

It's a fact: Robbie Knievel, son of Evel Knievel, jumped seven military aircraft on the deck of an aircraft-carrier in a stunt to promote the launch of a movie about his daredevil father.

ON THE EDGE

Born to Run

She's only four feet tall and weighs 46 pounds, but eight-year-old Zhang Huimin finished a 2,212-mile epic run across China in August 2007. Accompanied by her father, on a motorized bicycle, she jogged for 55 days. "She loves to run," said her dad, but observers are worried it could damage her young body.

Skater Boy

In August 2006, Dave Cornthwaite pushed off on his yellow board, "Elsa," for an extraordinary skateboard ride. He was freewheeling for charity across the blisteringly hot and arid continent of Australia. It took Dave almost five months to achieve his amazing 4,000-mile road trip from Perth to Brisbane.

Peak Fitness

"We don't want any casualties," announces the starter of the Tenzing-Hillary Everest Marathon. The cautious start is needed for the world's highest altitude race, which starts each May from close to Everest base camp at about 17,000 feet. Competitors walk and scramble 26.2 miles along packed ice and rickety swing bridges and descend nearly 6,000 feet.

Rhino Race

You have to be super fit to run the London or New York 26.2-mile marathons. So imagine jogging those city streets inside a very sweaty and smelly seven-foot rhinoceros suit. Step forward a group of runners intent on saving the rhino. Since 2000, they have raced in rhino costumes to raise money for the endangered species. Watch out for them charging in the next race.

79

WHO DARES?

Pole Plunge

Wearing only goggles, a cap, and swimming shorts, endurance swimmer Lewis Pugh strolled to the frozen edge and dove in. The water was icy, measuring 29°F, and Lewis was at the North Pole. Normally only polar bears or killer whales brave waters this cold, but in July 2007 Lewis became the first human being to swim a kilometer (just over half a mile) of the Arctic Ocean. He did it in 18 minutes and 50 seconds. Lewis copes with the extreme cold by using visualization techniques.

Ice Man

Karim Diab slipped into an ice hole in the frozen Moskva River in Moscow, Russia, in March 2005. After 60 minutes he emerged unable to talk, but just about able to smile. Most people can't stand such cold temperatures for longer than 20 minutes.

‹‹ Ripley Rewind ‹‹‹‹‹‹‹‹‹‹‹‹‹

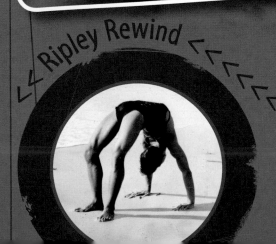

Crab Man

Will Pilot of Miami, Florida, crab-walked 25 miles in 8 hours 32 seconds. He didn't even stop to rest!

DANCE TILL YOU DROP

Rock climbing meets rhythmic dancing high up in the Nevada mountains or atop Seattle's Space Needle. The Bandaloop Dance Company, led by dancer Amelia Rudolph, is a group of aerial ballet dancers who perform synchronized somersaults, pirouettes, and freefall leaps with only ropes to secure them. In August 2003, they danced on a rock face 2,500 feet high beside the spectacular Yosemite Falls. The heady mix of dance, sport, and environment has attracted half a million spectators to their shows. Amelia says, "We all have a dream of floating, flying, and soaring," and she is certainly living that dream.

One trick involves freefalling for 11 seconds on a 275-foot-long rope.

So far the only injury to the dancers has been a stubbed toe and a slightly sore head.

flying

81

Write On

Calligraphy is an art dating back to the earliest days of history, and is practiced throughout China to this day. Translated, the word means good writing, and calligraphers are highly respected. It's an incredibly difficult art to master at any age, but Chen Xiaoyan could write the complicated symbols perfectly when she was just four years old.

Talented Teen

If you get bored with the music you hear all the time, why not write your own? Adam Lorincz did just that and didn't stop at one tune—he wrote an entire musical! He was just 14 years old when his 92-minute composition, *Star of the King*, was first performed in Hungary in 2002.

Junior DJ

Usually kids listen to adults on the radio, but with Kimberley Perez it was the other way around! She hosted her own four-hour Saturday afternoon radio show on the Los Angeles station KLAX 97.9 La Raza FM when she was just five years old!

Young Genius

Michael Kearney said his first words at age four months and at six months was able to tell his doctor, "I have an ear infection." He learned to read at ten months. When he was six years old he enrolled in college, graduating at age eight with an Associate of Science in Geology. He was just ten years old when he graduated with a degree in anthropology from the University of South Alabama.

Gifted Sisters

Lucy and Georgia Halcrow of New Zealand must be among the world's cleverest sisters. Six-year-old Lucy is the youngest member of the country's high-IQ society, Mensa, and can draw at a level five years above her age. Georgia, aged ten, is also a Mensa member and has already written a 20,000-word novel!

Reading Twins

At just three years old, Chinese twins Zhuang Zezheng and Zhuang Zefang could read adult newspapers and more than 80 books. The twins, who were born prematurely, could understand around 2,400 Chinese characters and nearly 1,000 English words.

Strong Boy

With a rope attached to his ponytail, Bruce Khlebnikov pulled a four-ton jet airplane along a runway in Moscow, Russia, when he was just 11 years old! Three years later, in 2004, he pulled an entire train with his hair, dragging cars weighing a total of 35 tons a distance of ten feet.

On High

Temba Tsheri from Nepal was just 15 years old in 2001 when she climbed the world's highest mountain—29,035-foot-high Mount Everest. What made her achievement all the more incredible was that the previous year she had lost five fingers as a result of frostbite.

It's a fact: Sergey Karjakin from the Ukraine became the world's youngest chess grandmaster in 2002, at the age of just 12 years and 7 months.

ADD ONS

Give Her a Hand

Claudia Mitchell became the first woman in the world to flex her "bionic" muscles. After losing her real arm in a motorcycle accident in 2004, she now controls her metal-and-wire version using her thoughts—just like a real limb. The ends of the nerves that once controlled her real arm were removed from her shoulder and then connected to nerves in her chest muscle. Electrodes fixed to a harness worn on the shoulder detect impulses from the nerves to the muscle. A tiny computer passes the information to the mechanical arm. Now Claudia can fold clothes, eat a banana, and wash the dishes.

It's a fact: Doctors believe that a patient whose organs have been damaged after a severe spinal nerve injury, could one day have his or her head transplanted onto a new body, supplying the patient with new organs.

Ear Ear

Janet Craven, from West Yorkshire, England, was born with no ears and was unable to hear. All that changed in February 2002, when she emerged from the hospital, after a complex operation combining metal pins and magnets, with two new surgically attached silicone ears. These and implanted hearing aids have revolutionized her life, she says.

Eye Wonder

In February 1941, Mrs. Epigmegnia Rodriguez, from Mexico City, gazed at the cameras and stunned the medical world. Her doctor, Angel Camargo, had successfully transplanted a cornea from a cat's eye onto Mrs. Rodriguez's right eye to improve her badly damaged vision.

Tongue in Cheek

Surgeons at Gliwice General Hospital, Poland, found a successful if unusual solution to replacing one man's damaged tongue. In August 2006, they removed 23-year-old Jarislav Ernst's cancer-ridden tongue and sewed in a new one made from the collected skin, fat, and nerve tissue of his buttocks.

NEW HEIGHTS

Up and Away

In July 2007, a Californian company advertised the first flying saucer for sale. Moller's M200G is really a compact hovercraft. The down draft of eight powerful engines creates a ten-foot lift, strong enough to carry you at 50 miles per hour over places where wheels cannot tread. However, sightings of the skycar flying remain rare.

Wonder Wall

In July 2005, Danny Way from San Diego, California, leapt the Great Wall of China—on a skateboard! Rolling down a 99-foot ramp—the biggest skateboard ramp ever constructed—Danny came close to 50 miles per hour to clear the Ju Yong Guan Gate. He was the first person to achieve this feat. Then he did it another four times, performing 360-degree spins just for effect.

Star Trekkin'

In June 2007, plans were unveiled to launch a space plane on a 90-minute flight. By 2012, tourists will be able to experience three minutes of weightlessness just below the Earth's orbit, at an altitude of 60 miles. For $265,000, it's an economy fare compared to the $25 million it costs space tourists to orbit with Russian Soyuz cosmonauts.

Johann Traber Sr. and Jr. share a highly dangerous double act. The father and son German duo perform death-defying high-wire stunts together. In May 2007, near the famous Frauenkirche (Church of Our Lady) in Munich, Germany, Johann Sr. motor-biked on a wire 130 feet aboveground while his son dangled below, trapeze-style.

Family Entertainment

<< Ripley Rewind <<<<<

Easy Does It

Clifford Calverley of Toronto, Canada, crossed Niagara Falls on a steel cable in 1892, taking just 6 minutes 32 seconds. He also managed to spin a ring on his legs while he did it.

It's a fact: American stunt expert Eric Scott reached a vertical height of 152 feet using a rocket belt around his waist and a jetpack on his back. He took off in the skies over London in 2004.

THEM AND US

Cat Call

In July 2003, a Japanese toy company launched a console that supposedly translates cat calls into human-speech. It's called the "Meowlingual." When a cat mews, the translator scans thousands of miaows on the device's database and sorts it into one of several key emotions—such as happy, sad, frustrated, needy. The console displays cute phrases matching that emotion.

High Flyer

Angelo d'Arrigo was called the "human condor" because he flew his hang glider beside these birds of prey high in the Andes Mountains in South America. He also paraglided beside Himalayan eagles near Mount Everest. By gliding without motors he could get close to supreme flyers and study their flight patterns close-up. He even crossed Siberia with Siberian cranes.

<< Ripley Rewind <<<<<<<

Family Fun

President Calvin Coolidge and his wife, Grace, had a pet racoon named Rebecca. Guests screeching at the wild animal in the White House never failed to make the president laugh.

COMPANY OF WOLVES

Shaun Ellis has lived and worked with wolves in captivity for so long that he now understands their behavior patterns. In fact he's so confident in their company that he's about to move in with a wild pack in Finland near the Russian border.

When a wolf is being **defensive**, it will **cover** its food with flattened ears, lift its lips, **growl**, and stick its tongue through its lips.

When living with a pack, he mimics the body language, facial expressions, and sounds of the wolves and aims to be accepted by each pack member. Says Shaun: "Any sound they make which is low in tone is discouraging, anything high is encouraging. Pulling the lips up gently to show the teeth is an action that can be used as a weapon. If I want to play the 'nanny' in the pack, my role is to diffuse tension, and I may have to put my head between two fighting wolves. I also have to eat the part of animal they've killed that is right for my position. A diffuser may have to eat the liver and heart."

grrr...

Double Trouble

Scott MacInnes became the first man on record in Alaska to survive two bear attacks. In 2005, he was out for his morning jog when he was savaged by a brown bear and suffered head, neck, and abdomen wounds—38 years after being the victim of a similar attack.

Tsunami Survivor

After the devastating Asian tsunami of 2004 washed away his home, an Indonesian man spent eight days at sea floating on a makeshift raft of tree branches. Rizal Sbahputra survived by drinking rainwater and eating floating coconuts, which he cracked open with a chainsaw he had found.

Shooting Shock

Wendell Coleman of Jacksonville, Florida, was mystified to wake up one morning with a headache and swollen lips. He went to the hospital, where doctors found a bullet embedded in his tongue! Coleman hadn't known he'd been shot!

Mud Trap

When a volcanic eruption wiped out the Colombian town of Armero in 1985, killing more than 20,000 people, Efrain Gómez Primo was trapped between wooden slats in water and mud that reached right up to his neck. As the mud ebbed and flowed, he was lost and rediscovered three times in the wake of the avalanche, before rescuers could finally free him.

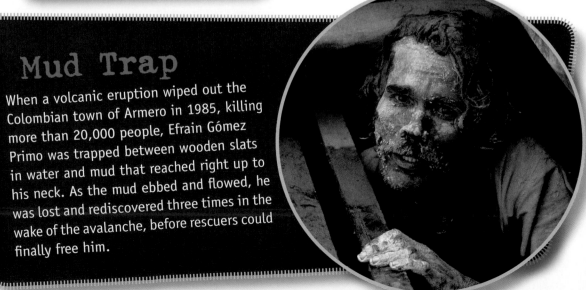

Pocket Atlas

Seeing his father, Rique, pinned under a car in 1984, nine-year-old Jeremy Schill from Jamestown, North Dakota, sprang into action. Even though he weighed only 65 pounds, Jeremy managed to lift the family's 4,000-pound Ford high enough for his dad to wriggle free.

Mirror Mirror

Hiker Lon McAdam spent six days lost in Arizona's Superstition Wilderness with a broken knee in 2007, but lived to tell the tale. He was in the middle of nowhere, he couldn't walk, his cell phone had broken in the fall, and no one was expecting him home for another week—but he managed to use a small mirror to attract a rescue helicopter.

Sharp Practice

Ouch! Not many people would be happy to land in a prickly blackberry bush, but Michael Holmes was. In fact it saved the life of the British skydiver, breaking his fall from 15,000 feet after his parachute had failed. Consequently, he escaped with just a punctured lung and a broken ankle from the jump on New Zealand's North Island in 2006.

Mighty Molars

After falling through the ice and into a freezing lake in February 2006, Hungarian skater Ani Zoltany survived by holding on to the broken ice with her teeth for ten minutes! As frostbite attacked her hands, the only way she could keep her head above water was to grip the ice with her teeth until help arrived.

It's a fact: Roy C. Sullivan, a Virginia forest ranger, survived seven lightning attacks between 1942 and 1977, losing nothing more than a toenail and his eyebrows. He became known as "The Human Lightning Rod."

NATURE OR NURTURE?

Glass Guzzler

Wang Chengke from Qingdao, China, has a taste for the unusual. The 24-year-old can eat glass and porcelain without any apparent harm. He has an extra-thick stomach lining and his stomach juices break down digested glass and porcelain five times faster than normal. By May 2007, he'd eaten more than a ton of glass.

Foot Note

To celebrate China's National Day on October 3, 2006, one man in a Shanghai park displayed curious skills to create his miniature masterpiece. He put together his delicately constructed mini-cycle—every nut, bolt, and spoke—using just one foot!

Tugging Teeth

"King of Teeth" Rathakrishnan Velu should bare his teeth and smile at his latest stunt. In August 2007, at Kuala Lumpur Station, Malaysia, he dragged nearly 300 tons of train over nine feet with his teeth! Zhang Xinquan of China pulled a similar stunt in June 2005, heaving a locomotive for 164 feet—with his ears.

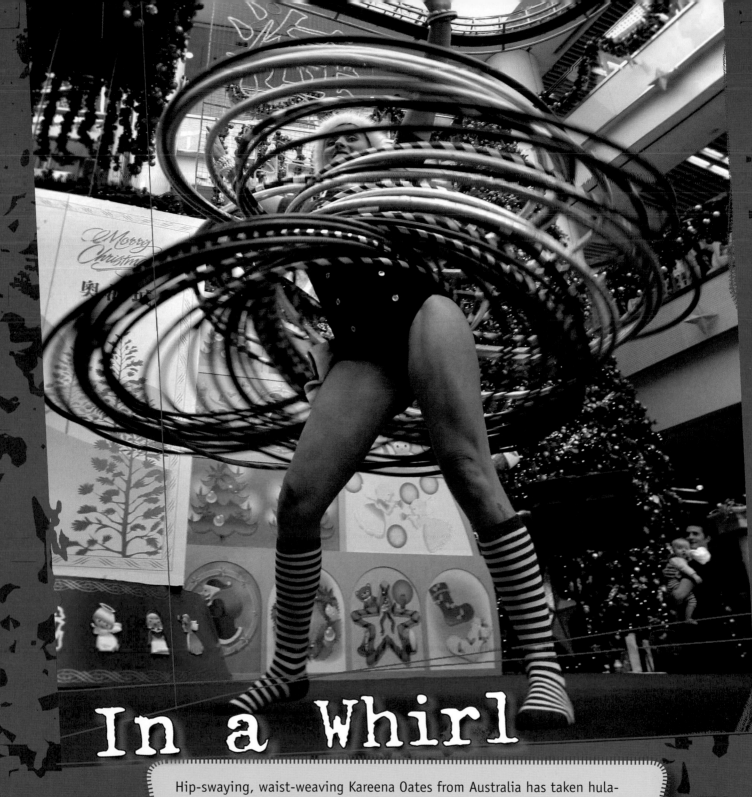

In a Whirl

Hip-swaying, waist-weaving Kareena Oates from Australia has taken hula-hooping to the edge. She can spin 100 hoops around her body, a feat she managed in June 2005, making her the first person to reach that figure. So get practicing and aim for 101.

A teenage Russian girl appears to have X-ray vision, which enables her to see inside human bodies. Natalia Demkina can describe the insides of bodies in detail, using her talent to diagnose medical conditions.

GIANT JOURNEYS

20

Million miles →

1 Between 2000 and 2003, Charles Veley visited 350 countries, enclaves, islands, federations, and territories, spending over $1 million on journeying almost a million miles. His most difficult destination was Clipperton Island, off the coast of Mexico. Because of a treacherous reef, his boat was unable to land, forcing him to swim to shore.

105,000 miles →

2 In May 2002, British couple Simon and Monika Newbound set off from Dublin, Ireland, on a monumental motorcycle journey that would take them more than three years to complete. By May 2005, the pair had logged visits to 54 countries and had ridden an amazing 105,000 miles.

3,900 miles

9 A French veterinary surgeon became the first person to cross the shark-infested Indian Ocean on a sailboard. Raphaela Le Gouvello of Brittany, France, landed on the island of Réunion, off the eastern coast of Africa, in June 2006, having completed a solo 3,900-mile voyage.

4,300 miles →

8 It took four British women—Sophia Cunningham, Lucy Kelaart, Alexandra Tolstoy, and Victoria Westmacott—eight months to ride horses and camels across Uzbekistan, Kygyzstan, and two-thirds of China, taking on four deserts and two mountain ranges.

3,500 miles →

10 Released in northern France in order to make the journey back to his loft in Liverpool, England, Billy, a homing pigeon, took a wrong turn and ended up in New York—a 3,500-mile journey!

2,000 miles   **1,500 miles** →

11 In April 2005, a British couple drove from the northern coast of Scotland, to the southern tip of Italy without getting out of their car. Dr. James Shippen and Barbara May made the journey using their Indipod, a toilet for inside the car.

12 In 1953, Sugar, a Persian cat, trekked 1,500 miles from Anderson, California, to Gage, Oklahoma, after her owners moved. The family had left the cat with a friend because of her bad hip, but Sugar made a 14-month journey to be reunited with them.

1,300 feet →

20 A mystery cat with a purple collar gets on a busy bus travelling from Walsall to Wolverhampton, England, at the same stop most mornings. He then jumps off at the next stop about 1,300 feet down the road, near a fish-and-chip shop.

8 miles →

19 Jake the Muscovy duck waddled for weeks to return to his sweetheart, Jemima. Her owner Roy Shindler had given Jake to a friend eight miles away. A month later, Jake reappeared at his old home.

20 miles →

18 In 2005, three elderly ladies took 24 hours to get home after becoming lost on their 20-mile journey home from church. It should have been a short drive home to Upson County, Florida.

47,224 miles

3

Canadian Jean Béliveau is on a 12-year walk around the world, covering 47,224 miles. He set off from Montreal on August 18, 2000, traveling with a three-wheeled stroller containing food, clothing, a first-aid kit, a small tent, and a sleeping bag, and aims to be back in Canada by 2012.

18,000 miles

4

Mohammed Salahuddin Choudhury and his wife Neena of Calcutta, India, went around the world by car in just 39 days in 1991.

14,500 miles

5

Gary Hatter of Champaign, Illinois, made a 14,500-mile journey around America—on a lawnmower! Leaving Portland, Maine, in May 2000, he passed through 48 U.S. states and dipped into Canada and Mexico before arriving at Daytona Beach, Florida, in February 2001.

13,000 miles

6

In June 2006, Adriaan Marais and Marinus Du Plessis set off on jet skis from Anchorage, Alaska, on a 13,000-mile trip to Miami, Florida. Their route took them down the west coast of the U.S., then through the Panama Canal to the east coast.

10,600 miles

7

In 2005, paraplegic Andreas Dagelet set out from Coochiemudlo Island, Brisbane, to circumnavigate Australia on a handcycle—a sort of bicycle that is powered by arms and hands instead of legs and feet. The entire journey measured approximately 10,600 miles.

105 miles

15

In the annual 105-mile, nonstop Desert Cup race across the arid desert of Jordan, participants carry all their own equipment and supplies—apart from drinking water. The competitors must complete the race in 60 hours.

250 miles

14

On August 27, 1933, Lieutenant Tito Falconi of the Italian Air Force flew a plane from St. Louis, Missouri, to Joilet, Illinois, a distance of 250 miles in 3 hours 6 minutes 30 seconds— flying upside down!

874 miles

13

In 1999, Hank Harp drove a motorized toilet the length of Britain. He sat on the seat of the chemical toilet, which was powered by an electric motor, and moved at a speed of four miles per hour.

62 miles

17

In September 2002, 84-year old grandmother Mary Murphy made the 62-mile, four-hour trip from Long Beach, California, to Catalina Island by hydrofoil water-skiing. She wanted to make the trip while still young enough!

70 miles

16

A cat that hitchhiked a ride on the underbelly of an S.U.V. in 2005 survived a 70-mile journey on the New Jersey Turnpike. The cat—nicknamed Miracle— was freed when a motorist spotted it through the S.U.V.'s wheel well and flagged down the driver.

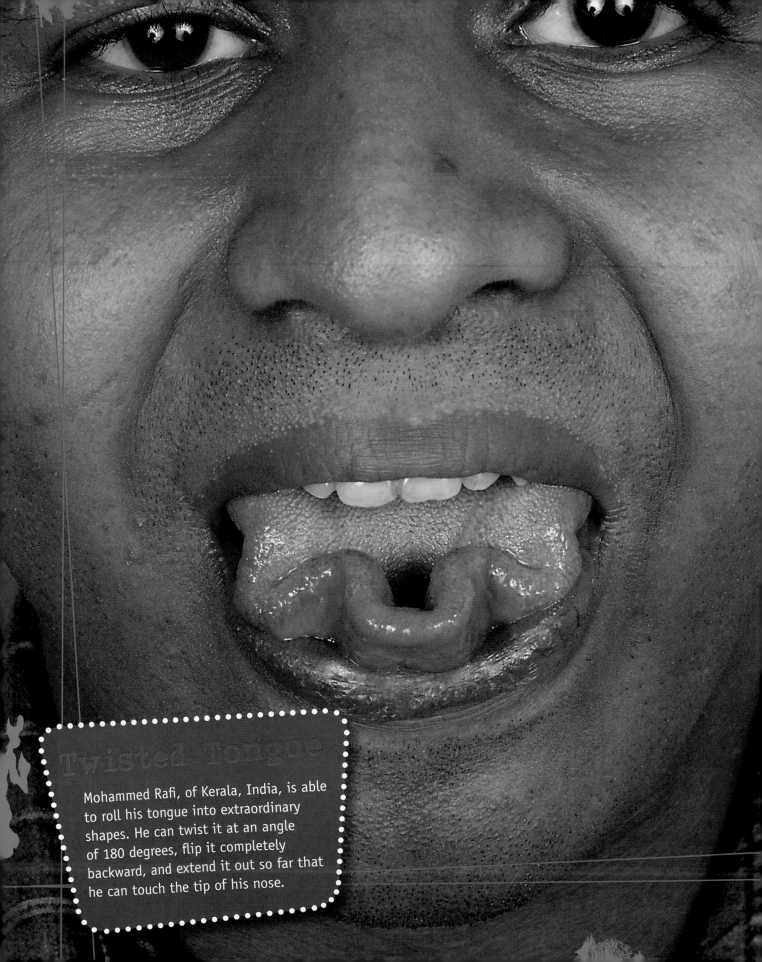

Twisted Tongue

Mohammed Rafi, of Kerala, India, is able to roll his tongue into extraordinary shapes. He can twist it at an angle of 180 degrees, flip it completely backward, and extend it out so far that he can touch the tip of his nose.

Chapter 5

BODY ODDITY

GENE JUGGLING

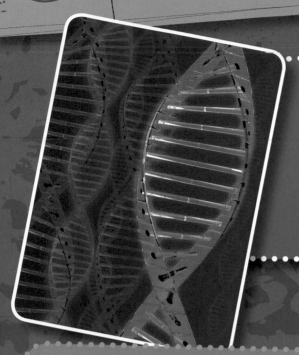

Double Helix Double

Despite giving birth, Karen Keegan received the news that a DNA test could not link her as the mother of her children. It was thought that she was a chimera, someone with two sets of DNA. To prove that she was the mother of her children, doctors had to find the second set of DNA in her body—the DNA she'd passed onto her children—and finally tracked it down in her thyroid gland.

Body Talk

Rose Siggins has half a body but a full-size life. She is the proud mom of two children and loves re-building cars, including a 1968 Mustang, which she plans to race. Rose from Pueblo, Colorado, was born without a pelvis and a section of her spine is missing. She had both legs amputated when she was two years old. She moves around on her hands, and often on a skateboard.

Ripley Rewind ‹‹ ‹‹ ‹‹ ‹‹ ‹‹

Family Man

Eli Bowan was born without legs, only feet. He was married and was the father of a large family.

Made to Measure

"I'm just an average Ukrainian farmhand," jokes Leonid Stadnyk, who towers over everybody else in his country. He's 8 feet 4 inches tall and has massive feet to match. So he really appreciated German shoemaker Georg Wessels when Georg presented him with a pair of hiking shoes to fit his 17-inch feet, at his home village of Podolyantsi in May 2005.

It's a fact: In 2003, composer Richard Krull and researchers Aurora Sanchez Sousa and Fernando Baquero of Ramon y Cajal Hospital in Madrid, Spain, turned DNA sequences into music and recorded a CD.

HELLO BABY

Two Tone

Mother Kylee Hodgson couldn't quite believe her eyes: one of her baby twins, Remee, was white, while Kian, born a minute later, was black. The twins were born at Queen's Medical Centre, Nottingham, England, in April 2005. Kylee and her partner Remi are both biracial, but the twins' skin tones were a surprise.

It's a fact: The city of Cali in Colombia hosted a crawling marathon for babies in 2006—and more than 1,100 babies took part. Infants aged between 8 and 18 months were eligible and they crawled along a 16-foot track.

Girl Power

Tatyana Khalina shocked her husband and hospital staff by giving birth to a 17-pound baby girl, Nadia, in September 2007 in Barnaul, Siberia. That's about the same size as a six-month-old child and more than double an average newborn's weight.

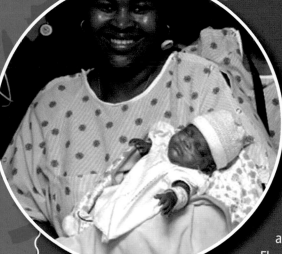

Tiny Tot

Amillia Sonja Taylor became a celebrity in October 2006. She was born weighing only 10 ounces, and was no longer than a ballpoint pen! Babies under 14 ounces were once thought to have no chance of survival, so her successful birth and survival at Baptist Hospital, Miami, Florida, is a medical marvel.

Multiple Miracle

Nkem Chukwu made medical history in Houston, Texas. In December 1998 she gave birth to eight tiny babies—the first octuplets born in the U.S.A. The six girls and two boys weighed only 10 pounds in total—not much more than one average baby. Sadly, one little girl did not survive, but the other seven are all healthy children.

HOW OLD?

Fit for Life

So you thought bodybuilding was just for the young? Meet Billy Fraser who is 69, with the oiled pecs and biceps of a much younger man. Bodybuilding is said to be one of the fastest-growing activities among men and women over 60, and aging gracefully now involves pumping iron, all-day workouts, and spray-on tans. In California, there's even a competition for bodybuilders over 70. So all the squats, pushups, and bench presses can keep you fit *and* famous.

Weight Watcher

When he was born, Zack Strenkert, from Bloomingburg, New York, weighed a normal 10 pounds 12 ounces. But, by the time he had reached the age of 17 months (shown here in June 1996), Zack weighed in at nearly 68 pounds, as much as an average eight or nine year old! He was three feet tall, his T-shirts were size 14, and his ankles didn't fit into shoes. Zack has a rare genetic disorder called Simpson Golabi Behmel Syndrome, which means he eats normally and puts on excess weight and height.

AGE MATTERS

John Tacket, from Bay City in Michigan, suffered from a disease so rare it's virtually impossible to study.

People with progeria seem to age 5 to 10 times what's usual.

At any one time in the U.S., less than a dozen children have the "rapid aging" disease progeria. By going public with his condition, John, photographed here when he was just 15, allowed doctors to research and discover why it afflicts so very few children. In April 2003 a team of American and French scientists discovered that a defective gene lying deep inside a single cell is linked to progeria. "We're looking forward to the second step—a cure or a treatment," said John. Sadly, he did not live to see the development of the cure he so bravely championed.

OUCH!

Keeping Track

Proving you're a strong man takes all sorts of tests of strength and endurance. For Jagga Singh, from Punjab, India, it's being ridden over by giant tractor tires. Jagga showed his skills in February 2005 at the Kila Raipur Rural Olympics.

Toughing It Out

Each year some 5,000 courageous competitors run possibly the most demanding assault course in the world. Athletes at the twice-annual Tough Guy Challenge in Perton, England, hot-foot it through flames, wade through mud, drag themselves through underwater tunnels, and go up and down numerous rope climbs, before plunging into icy water. Founder Billy Wilson says, "It's all about facing your fears."

It's a fact: Eric Morris of Port Orchard, Washington, regularly wrestles giant Pacific octopuses in Puget Sound and at the World Octopus Wrestling Championships each year in Tacoma, Washington.

Hammer Head

During May Day festivities in China, anything goes—including taking a hammer to bricks balanced on someone else's head and smashing them to smithereens. Happily, there were no permanently injured heads during this controlled "fun" in Kaifeng, China, in May 2005.

Ripley Rewind

Weight for It

Habu the Iron-Tongued Man could lift a large cylinder weighing 105 pounds with a hook through his tongue.

BODY WORK

Connect the Dots

Gone are the days when a simple daisy tattoo would do. Anil Gupta, working in New York City, can tattoo reproductions of old masters without losing any detail. Clients can opt for a four-centimeter tattoo of Seurat's "Sunday Afternoon on the Island of La Grande Jatte," shown here, or have Leonardo da Vinci's "The Last Supper" copied across their back.

Ear Shot

Venezuelan extreme tattooist Constantino showed up in Caracas in January 2006 with a little extra something. Not happy with a stud earring, which most people would settle for, he was sporting a glass cup supported by a hole in his ear lobe.

Mission: Lizard

Erik Sprague is a man with a mission. A mission to look like a reptile, that is! He's known as the Lizardman for a reason. His extensive body modifications include tattooed scales, filed teeth, a surgically split tongue, and a bony ridge set into his forehead.

Here's Looking at You

Is this really someone with three eyes, two noses, and two mouths? Seen close up, it's complicated, but from a distance the whole picture is clearer. This is body art from Laura Spector. In April 2001, in a New York department store window, she cleverly copied a painting onto her husband Chadwick Gray's body.

The Enigma, for many years a member of The Jim Rose Circus, has his entire body covered with a blue jigsaw-puzzle tattoo. The American performer has also had horns implanted in the skin on his skull!

Tongue Vision

Mike Ciarciello can "see" using his tongue. Mike has been blind since birth but in 2006 researchers at Canada's University of Montreal mounted a small camera on his forehead, which sent electrical impulses about what it saw to a small grid placed on his tongue. Consequently, he was able to walk through a complicated obstacle course without a cane.

Wide Awake

How about going 34 years without any sleep! A 65-year-old Vietnamese farmer, Hai Ngoc, hasn't slept since getting a fever in 1973—that's more than 12,000 consecutive sleepless nights. He's still healthy, however, and proves it every day by carrying two 110-pound bags of fertilizer down 2½ miles of road.

King Burp

Paul Hunn, of Enfield, England, can do a burp of 118 decibels—that's a similar volume to a pneumatic drill or to what you'd hear if you stood 100 yards from a jet engine taking off! He trains by eating curries and kebabs and drinking plenty of carbonated drinks.

Eye Popper

Since the age of nine, Jalisa Mae Thompson, from Atlantic City, New Jersey, has been able to pop her eyeballs beyond her eye sockets. "I started popping my eyes out by sticking my finger at the top of my eye and pushing," she says. Now she can do it at will. She won the Funny Face Contest at the Ripley's Museum in Atlantic City in 2006.

Ripley's
Believe It or Not!
Atlantic City, NJ

Rate of Inflation

Most people would inflate a balloon by putting it in their mouth and blowing—but not Zhang Yingmin, from China's Shandong Province. He can blow up balloons by expelling air from his eyes and ears! He holds his nose, takes a breath, and blows through a pipe in his ear and one over his eye.

In a Twist

You never know whether Bitu Gandhi is coming or going, because he can walk with his heels twisted backward! Inspired by an item on the *Ripley's Believe It or Not!* TV show, the Indian teenager from Rajkot practiced all day and all night for a year until he was able to walk 300 steps forward and 300 steps backward by twisting his ankles almost 180 degrees. Now some of his neighbors are practicing daily with him.

Wick-ed!

There's a man in China whose eyes are so amazingly strong that he can blow out candles with them. Using a specially made pair of glasses with air tubes attached, Yu Hongqua is able to create enough air to extinguish a burning flame, leaving just the wick smoldering.

Thunder Clap

Give this man a standing ovation. When Zhang Quan claps his hands it's like a clap of thunder. The man from China has had his clapping measured at 107 decibels—that's almost as loud as the sound of a helicopter's blades.

It's a fact:

Every night while you're asleep, you grow by about 0.3 inches, but shrink again in the morning. This is because pressure on the cartilage disks in the spine is relieved during sleep, allowing the disks to expand.

HAIR AND NOW

Eerie!

B.D. Tyagi, from Bhopal, India, has hair strands growing from his ears that are four inches long! Do you think he can 'ear anything? Maybe he should contact Nina Sparre, of Vamhuf, Sweden, who practices *Haarkulla*, or "Hair Farming," creating art and clothing out of human hair.

Long Locks

Dai Yueqin, from China has not cut her hair for 28 years! In April 2007 it reached a length of 14 feet 1 inch. A single hair can reach a length of just over 16 feet before it falls out, so hers will keep growing for a while yet.

A Cut Above

During the Cricket World Cup 2007, Indian cricket fan Bhola Sarder had his head shaved in the shape of a cricket match to show his support.

Strong Strands

Who would think that one strand of human hair is as strong as an iron strand of the same diameter? To prove the point, Ganesh Bhagat Chourasia, from Calcutta, can suspend ten bricks weighing 77 pounds from his moustache. More hair-raising still, in 1931, "Little Giant" Eddie Polo pulled a car 100 yards in 1 minute 40 seconds in Dover, New Hampshire—using just his ponytail.

It's a fact: J.M. Thompson of Philadelphia managed to drill holes measuring 0.0007 inch in diameter through a human hair. And Howard Adam of Wisconsin even threaded a hair through a hair!

NEW AGE

Rock 'n' Old

Loud music is for teens—or was until The Zimmers came along. Named after a special frame that aids senior citizens who have trouble walking, The Zimmers, who are nearly all over 90 years old, make up possibly the oldest rock band in the world. In April 2007 they recorded a cover version of the youth anthem "My Generation" by The Who. The pop single (its CD cover is shown here) was released in the U.K. to draw attention to how society can neglect old people of "their generation." The Zimmers, including Winnie, who at the time was 99 years old and Buster aged 100, have now become an unlikely pop sensation: "I feel the experience has brought me back to life," said lead singer Alf Carretta, who was 90 years young at the time.

Oldest Winger in Town

While many older people enjoy gardening or golf, Tom Lackey likes to get airborne. In May 2006 Tom became the oldest person, at 84, to wing-walk. At an airfield in Warwickshire, England, he strapped in atop a specially adapted stunt aircraft. The plane and Tom revved through loop-the-loops and victory rolls. Tom's tricks are even more remarkable because, after suffering a stroke, he can only walk aided by two sticks. "I ride a plane easier than I walk," he laughed.

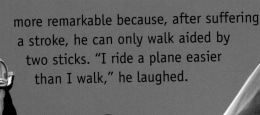

TOP MAN

At the sprightly age of 71 years, 2 months and 2 days, Katsusuke Yanagisawa achieved his dream. The retired junior high school teacher (in the foreground in the photograph) became the oldest person ever to scale the summit of Mount Everest. Exhausted, out of breath, and feeling numb from the biting winds, Katsusuke reached the top of the world's highest peak, at 29,035 feet, in May 2007. "I didn't think I would make it" he gasped and added, "I do feel relieved."

Everest has claimed more than 200 lives since it was first scaled in 1953.

He has a right to feel that way, because this is the ultimate achievement for even a young mountaineer at peak fitness. This senior citizen was six months older than the previously oldest climber, who was also Japanese.

scaling
new heights

BRILLIANT BODIES

Write Stuff

Sometimes a hand can ache if it's been holding a pen and writing too long. That's not a problem for Tapan Dey, from India, however, because he can write a poem with a pen clipped to his hair. He can also put pen to paper using his nose and ear, as well as both hands—all at the same time.

Finger-lickin' Good

Yassir El Hammud was born in Berlin, Germany, in March 2006 with six fingers on each hand, plus 11 toes! His extra toe has been removed so he can start learning to walk.

Nailing It

It has taken Li Jianping, of Shishi City, China, 15 years to grow the curly nails on his left hand. Their current total length is three feet, but it's an achievement that comes with a price. To avoid breaking a nail, he never goes to crowded places, and he admits, "I have to sleep with my left wrist under my head to prevent it moving."

<< Ripley Rewind <<<<<<<<

Bendy Body

At age 17, Jaqueline Terry, of Montgomery, Alabama, could perform this rare and difficult jaw balance.

It's a fact: Double-thumbed cotton picker R.L. Stubblefield from Italy, Texas, had two thumbs on his right hand, which enabled him to pick an amazing 300 pounds of cotton a day during the 1930s.

BODY BONANZA

1
The body sheds and re-grows about 100 scalp hairs and five eyelashes every day.

4
The stomach has to produce a new layer of mucus every two weeks—otherwise it would digest itself.

5
The only internal part of the body that grows continually throughout life is the eye lens.

2
An average man's beard would grow to a length of 30 feet in his lifetime, provided he never trimmed or shaved it.

3
Approximately two thirds of an average person's body weight is made up of water.

19
Our bodies are constantly recreating themselves—we renew the cells in our skeleton every three months and in our skin every month.

17
In the human eye, all images are transmitted to the retina upside down and the brain turns them right way up. A newborn baby sees the world upside down, because it takes a while for the brain to learn how to do this.

20
Every second, the human body creates 15 million new red blood cells and kills 15 million old ones.

18
Within a tiny drop of blood, there are around five million red blood cells, 300,000 platelets, and 10,000 white blood cells.

16
About 75 percent of household dust is made up of dead skin flakes.

6

Your eyes will always be the same size they were at birth, but your nose and ears will never stop growing.

8

If these parts of the human body were straightened out and joined together, they would be this long:

- *Nerves, including micro-nerves—99,422 miles (almost halfway to the Moon)*
- *Blood vessels—60,000 miles (twice around the Earth)*
- *Nephrons (tiny tubes in the kidneys)—over 62 miles*
- *Sweat gland tubules—31 miles*

9

Did you know that girls have more taste buds than boys?

7

Fingernails grow four times faster than toenails.

10

When a person sneezes, the heart and all bodily functions momentarily stop.

11

The average human brain weighs just three pounds and is amazingly complex. The total memory capacity of the brain is around 100 trillion bits of data, which is equivalent to the information in 500,000 large multi-volume encyclopedias, or, in computer terms, about 1,000 gigabytes.

14

Skin is the body's largest organ, weighing just over seven pounds. It would occupy about 20 square feet if spread out.

13

If all the hairs grown all over the body in one year were added together they would measure more than 12 miles in length.

15

At birth, the human body has 300 bones, but an adult has only 206. This is because some of a baby's tiny bones fuse together.

12

A sneeze travels out of your mouth at more than 100 miles per hour.

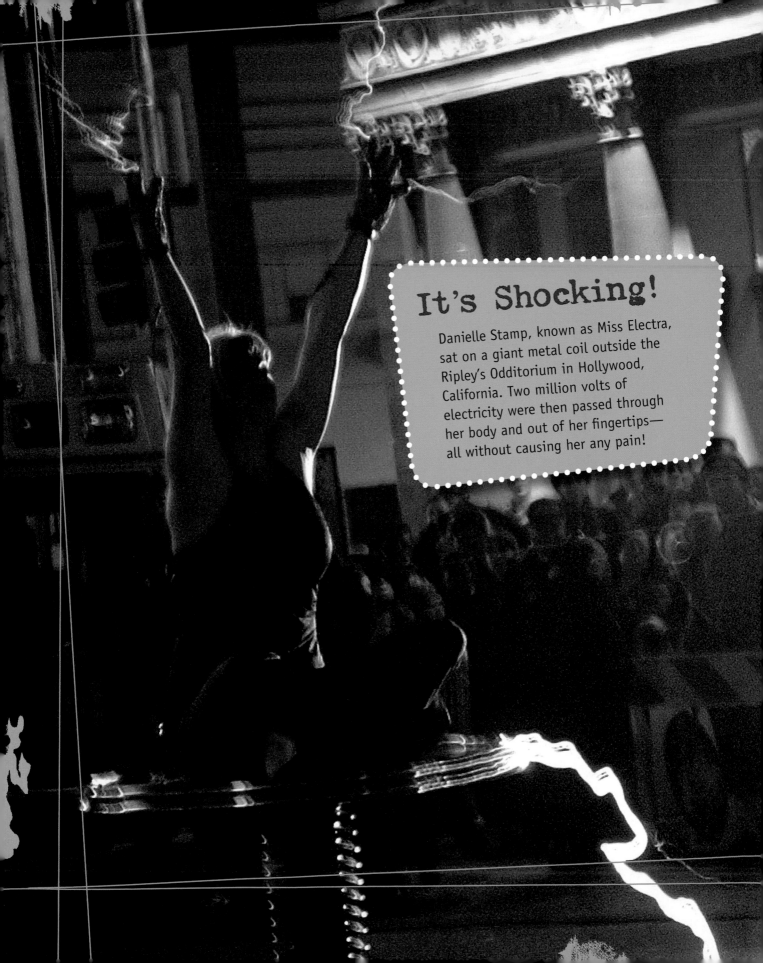

It's Shocking!

Danielle Stamp, known as Miss Electra, sat on a giant metal coil outside the Ripley's Odditorium in Hollywood, California. Two million volts of electricity were then passed through her body and out of her fingertips— all without causing her any pain!

Chapter 6
STRANGE BUT TRUE

THAT'S FREAKY

Foxy Behavior

A fox got more than it bargained for when it started to nose around a discarded car wheel. Its head got completely caught inside the rim. Simon Cowell from Surrey, England, found the cub in his back yard in May, 2007. Fortunately wildlife volunteers were able to free the fox, who suffered no ill effects.

Bouncing Back

Eddie Szula, photographed here in 1942, is a true survivor. The parachute jumper's chute failed to open on a jump on July 26, 1941. He plummeted 2,000 feet, bounced four feet into the air on landing, and never lost consciousness.

Good Luck Arm

One woman in Lanzhou, China, woke up one morning in August 2005 to find the words "good luck" had mysteriously appeared on her right arm. She couldn't understand how the characters had formed, and neither could the doctors who studied the writing.

Kneedy Grandmother

Amia Fore was checking in the mirror one day when she noticed what appeared to be a face on her right kneecap. She took some pictures and showed them to her spiritual advisor, who believed it was Amia's first unborn grandchild. Amia was told that once the grandchild came into the world, the features would go away. Later, another face appeared on her other knee, the features appearing more detailed as weeks went by.

It's a fact

Don Karkoss, from New York, was blinded by shrapnel in 1942. He was head-butted in the same spot by a horse in December 2004 and miraculously began to see again.

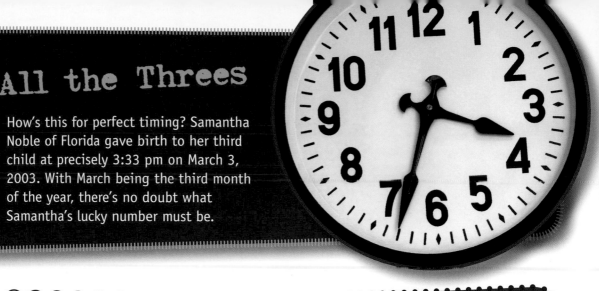

WHAT A COINCIDENCE!

All the Threes

How's this for perfect timing? Samantha Noble of Florida gave birth to her third child at precisely 3:33 pm on March 3, 2003. With March being the third month of the year, there's no doubt what Samantha's lucky number must be.

Ring Cycle?

Linda Blardo lost her high-school ring when she went swimming near her home in Zephyrhills, Florida. The ring was recovered in a Georgia state park 34 years later, 470 miles away. Nobody has any idea how it traveled quite so far.

Happy Return

Helen Swisshelm's Christmas present for 2001 was one she had always dreamed of—the class ring she had lost 53 years earlier! She had last seen it in 1948 while swimming in the Hudson River near her home in Cohoes, New York, but over half a century later, it was found by a man with a metal detector and traced to her via initials on the ring.

Lucky Find

When he lost his wallet on a mountaineering trip in Colorado in 1958, Paul Thiel gave up hope of it ever being found. Over 48 years later the wallet and its contents—including his driver's license, a fishing permit, a train ticket, and a $10 bill, all in good condition—were returned to him at his home in Kirkwood, Missouri. The wallet had been found beneath melted snow.

Day to Remember

If you're a member of the Steindl family from Brisbane, Australia, there's no excuse for forgetting a birthday. That's because four generations of the family were born on the same day—August 1. Norma Steindl was born on that day in 1915, her son Leigh in 1945, Leigh's daughter Suzanna in 1973, and Suzanna's son Emmanuel on August 1, 2003.

Crooked Crustacean

Losing his wallet during a swim in the sea, Paul Westlake of Plymouth, England, resigned himself to never seeing it again. A few days later it was returned to him—a deep-sea diver found it in the claws of a lobster on the ocean floor!

Unlucky Breaks

Eight-year-old twins Cassidy and Marissa Wiese of Laurel, Nebraska, both had roller-skating accidents on the same day in April 2004 that resulted in each breaking their left arm. Cassidy broke her arm at a friend's birthday party, and five hours later Marissa fell while demonstrating her skating skills to her mom. Naturally the girls wore matching blue casts.

Friends Reunited

Two friends who each thought the other had been killed during the Second World War were reunited 60 years later—after becoming next-door neighbors. Gilbert Fogg and Tom Parker were wounded on the same Italian battlefield in 1944 and lost touch, until Fogg moved into a house in Lincolnshire, England, and found his old friend living next door.

It's a fact: Three American presidents have died on Independence Day, July 4. John Adams and Thomas Jefferson both died on July 4, 1826, and James Monroe died on July 4, 1831.

NO WAY!

Cool Coats

It gets very humid for workers in Japan in mid-summer. So they may warm to this new "cool" jacket. Air-conditioned jackets were tested for the first time in August 2007, near Tokyo. They have two small fans run by rechargeable batteries sewn into the backs to provide a breeze.

124

It's a fact: Derek Paravichini of Surrey, England, has an amazing ability. The blind autistic boy can remember and store every tune he hears and play it back on the piano. He's been storing songs since he was two.

Blind Date

Candlelit dinners may become a thing of the past if a new fad for dining in the dark takes off. In December 2006, diners at a West Hollywood restaurant enjoyed a three-course gourmet meal served by blind waiters in a pitch-black room. We don't know how much food ended up on the floor.

Pandering to the Customer

A Chinese wildlife center that manages the waste of 60 pandas every day supplied an unusual 2008 Beijing Olympics souvenir—panda dung. A store in Chengdu sells trinkets and ornaments made from the droppings of these bamboo-chewing mammals that are iconic symbols of the host country.

<< Ripley Rewind <<<<<<<<

Match That!

Using no artificial support, 6,300 matches were placed on a bottle by Jean Phipps, Carrie Welling, Dick Lightcap, and Dorothy Taylor in Pittsburgh, Pennsylvania.

STRANGE LIVES

Jungle Bungle

In February 1972, on landing at Tokyo Airport, Shoichi Yokoi became a curious celebrity. "It is with much embarrassment that I have returned alive," announced the Japanese soldier. Shoichi had just been found in a cave in the jungles of Guam. He'd hidden there when American troops recaptured the island in 1944. The war ended in 1945, but Shoichi had no idea and continued his concealment for an amazing 28 years. He was discovered quite by chance by two islanders checking their fishing nets nearby.

Going Underground

Cave dwelling is not just a prehistoric pastime. The inhabitants of the opal-mining town of Coober Pedy in Australia also like living underground. The deep, dark caverns keep them cool against the scorching desert sun. Many of the residents are ex-miners, and their homes are converted mines with modern conveniences. There is even an underground bar and church. The Miao people near Ziyun, China, have a subterranean village in a 750-foot-long cave.

LOST IN TRANSIT

Mehran Karimi Nasseri's home isn't exactly his castle—it's more like his trolley. Mehran is a refugee who left Iran in August 1988, and landed at Charles de Gaulle Airport, Paris, France. Each time he tried to seek refuge in a new European country, he was sent back to Terminal One of this airport to await a successful application. It never came, so Mehran made the transit lounge his home.

His daily routine followed that of the terminal: up at 5 a.m., when the first passengers started to arrive, then a wash in the public bathrooms. He hung out on the curved seats near the shops with two luggage trolleys and an odd assortment of boxes and bags, spending time reading newspapers and writing his diary. His diary became a successful book— *The Terminal Man*.

A 2004 movie, *The Terminal*, starring Tom Hanks was also inspired by his sensational stopover.

He **lived** among the boutiques and restaurants of the departure area for over **16 years**, until August 2006 when he had to go into the hospital.

CURIOUS CURES

Up in Smoke

With a walnut over one eye, and dry moxa plant leaves lit and placed in both ears, this patient at a hospital in Jinan, China, looks very relaxed. He was undergoing traditional Chinese medicine in June 2007 to cure a condition where the muscles on the face had become temporarily paralyzed.

Fishy Practice

Every year in June, the Bathini Goud Brothers attract thousands of patients to their mobile hospital in Hyderabad, India. They come to take the brothers' fish medicine for breathing problems such as asthma. However, the remedy isn't so easy to swallow. It's a live slippery fish that has to go down in one gulp!

Ripley Rewind

Tough Guy

Sioux Indian chief Couzzingo, from Oxford, Ohio, broke one of his ribs, but instead of going to a hospital he performed some DIY surgery. He fastened his broken rib to his breastbone using a screwdriver without an anaesthetic.

Bee Patient

Take two live bees, place them either side of the nostrils, and let them sting! It sounds painful—and it is—but that's the treatment for some patients at a clinic in Xi'an, Central China. The bee venom is believed by some traditional Chinese doctors to reduce the swelling of an inflamed nose.

It's a fact: Derek Glover from Lincolnshire, England, was deaf for 15 years until he went on a ski holiday. He heard a loud "pop" while 7,000 feet up on a ski lift in the Italian mountains, and could hear perfectly again.

Go Green

In June 2007, Canadian doctor Alana Flexman was in the operating theater. She expected to see red blood from her patient but was startled when a dark green fluid trickled out instead— "the color of an avocado skin," she reported. The patient had been taking excessive doses of a medication for migraines, and this had caused his blood to turn green—the same color as Mr. Spock's Vulcan blood in *Star Trek*.

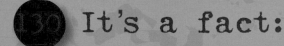

It's a fact: A ten-month-old girl with breathing problems was found to have a blade of grass growing on her lung. Surgeons in Zhengzhou, China, removed the grass and the girl recovered. Doctors think she swallowed a seed.

Lead in Head

Margret Wegner suffered from severe headaches and nosebleeds for 55 years. "It hurt like crazy," she says. The "it" was a pencil that pierced her skin and disappeared into her head when she fell over at age four. Only in August 2007 did doctors in Berlin, Germany, feel confident enough to extract the three-inch pencil without physical damage to Margaret.

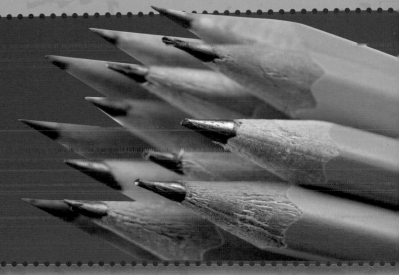

Knife Thief

When veterinarian Jon-Paul Carew looked at this X-ray he could hardly believe his eyes—a puppy aged six months had somehow swallowed a 13-inch serrated knife! Jane Scarola had been using a knife to carve a turkey at her home in Plantation, Florida, in September 2005. She put the blade on the counter away from the edge, but thinks that one of her six other dogs must have snatched it. From there it came into the possession of Elsie, her inquisitive St. Bernard puppy, who swallowed it!

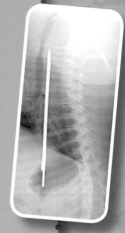

<< Ripley Rewind <<<<<<<<<

Hair Raising

Walter Albert of Lexington, Kentucky, was blond until he had a blood transfusion and his hair turned red and wavy.

131

ANCIENT SECRETS

Wizard Hat

Wizards actually did wear tall, pointed hats. That's what German archaeologists think after concluding that a series of golden cone-shaped objects unearthed in Europe over the past two centuries are actually hats. The headgear is decorated with astrological symbols that may have helped predict the movement of the sun and stars.

Temple Mystery

A 3,000-year-old hieroglyph in the Temple of Abydos in Egypt shows the outline of a helicopter as well as a submarine. Could the ancient Egyptians have possessed such craft or did they meet aliens? Skeptics say the patterns are a combination of erosion and adjustments to the original inscriptions.

Aztec Astronaut

Did inhabitants of a distant planet visit Earth hundreds or thousands of years ago? Experts say an Aztec carving, on display at the International UFO Museum and Research Center at Roswell, New Mexico, appears to depict an ancient astronaut. Or could there be another explanation?

Hare Care

Experts in Devon, England, are trying to unravel the mystery of a series of ancient symbols found in 17 local churches. The strange symbol—depicting three hares joined at the ears—could be connected to hitherto unknown trading links with China from 1,500 years ago, because in China there are 16 caves painted with the same motif.

Hidden Meaning

Housed at Yale University, the Voynich Manuscript is a 500-year-old relic written in a language that nobody has ever seen before. The manuscript, which contains 240 of the original 272 pages, was originally discovered in 1912 at a library in Rome, but until someone is able to decipher the text, we'll never know what it means.

Alien Visit

In 1938, in a remote cave high in the Himalayas, a Chinese archaeologist discovered 716 stone plates, dating back some 12,000 years. According to one interpretation, the hieroglyphics on the disks (known as the Dropa Stones) tell the story of the first visit of an alien civilization to our planet—by small, thin beings with large heads.

Mystery of the Deep

In 1964 the research vessel *Eltanin* discovered a mysterious structure 13,500 feet down on the bottom of the Atlantic Ocean, south of Cape Horn. It was described as a pole rising from the ocean floor with a series of 12 spokes attached. Some people think the *Eltanin* Antenna is an unknown marine life-form, but others believe it was put there, either by an ancient civilization or by beings from another world.

Island Script

Rongorongo is the hieroglyphic script used by early inhabitants of Easter Island in the Pacific Ocean. The language disappeared from use and now exists only on 26 pieces of wood in various museums across the world. It could hold the secret of how Polynesian people lived hundreds of years ago.

It's a fact: The Ancient Greeks passed on secret messages via tattoos drawn on their shaved heads. As the hair grew, the message was hidden, only to be revealed when the head was shaved again.

THEY'RE TAKING OVER

Say Cheese

Can a robot smile? Scientists think Kansei can. In June 2007 this robot demonstrated 36 different facial expressions at Meiji University, Tokyo, Japan. Type a keyword into its software and it scans half a million words. The face then responds with the appropriate look.

Robo-Twin

One is real flesh and blood, the other is a robot replica. Zou Renti, from Xi'an, China, has created a fully operational "clone" of himself. In fact, he has made more than 400 lifelike robots, including his Mr. Zou look-alike seen here at a robotics conference in Beijing in October 2006.

Super-fly Spy

Heard the buzz on the new breed of super spy? In July 2007 scientists at Harvard University launched their Robo-Fly. The fly-size mechanical insect weighing just 0.002 ounces can flap its wings at 110 beats per second. One day, its inventors think it could be used by the military as a snoop.

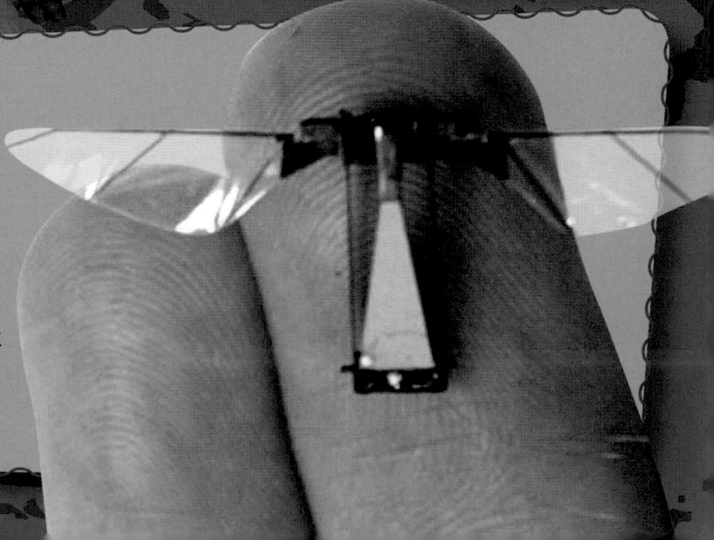

New Cops
on the Block

A 6-foot-7-inch electronic police officer was installed in June 2007 to monitor movements at a railway station in Wuhan, China. The robotic cop has four built-in cameras to keep an eye on law and order, and send out the right signals—it includes a panic alarm button—to would-be crooks.

It's a fact: Artificial intelligence researcher David Levy has claimed that humans and cyborgs will one day marry, as people search for the perfect partner. He says we have learned to love robotic pets, so it's just a matter of time.

IT'S ALL TRUE

Happy Tail

Fuji the dolphin loves to leap out of the water, but her aerial antics in July 2007 were propelled by an artificial tail. Vets on the Japanese island of Okinawa attached the rubber flukes after Fuji's real ones became diseased.

Puppy Love

A chihuahua named Heart-kun was born in May 2007 in Odate, Japan. What makes him lovable is his fur's unique brown pattern in the shape of a heart. Emiko Sakurada, the dog lover who bred the puppy, said she'd never seen such markings before and couldn't bear to part with him.

<< Ripley Rewind <<<<<<<<

Heads Up

This horse, owned by J.F. Daniel and R.L. Anderson of Craigsville, Virginia, had a marking on its neck in the shape of a Native American head.

Love Birds

鸾凤和鸣

Pelicans Pangpang and Yuanyuan got hitched in a showy ceremony in April 2007, at a zoo in Fuzhou, China. Staff helpers wanted to encourage the spotted-billed pelican male to accept his new mate after his first partner had died. It seemed to work. The happy couple hit it off straight away.

It's a fact: Did you know that if grasshoppers were the size of people they could leap the length of a basketball court?

MATH PATH

20

Use your knowledge about this book (and a little help from the index) to solve Ripley's crazy calculation. Hint: there's a significant date in the answer!

1 The number of worms buried with Mark Hogg

÷

2 The weight, in ounces, of Amillia Sonja Taylor at birth

+

3 The weight, in pounds, of the colossal squid found in February 2007

9 The number of beats per minute one yogi can force his heart to make

+

10 The number of toes Des the cat has

+

11 The number of years Hai Ngoc has gone without sleep

+

12 The age Katsusuke Yanagisawa was when he first scaled Everest

+

13 The number of girls born in the Chukwu octuplets

✕

The number of minutes Karim Diab stayed in an ice hole

14

+

20 The length, in inches, of the pencil lodged in Margret Wegner's head for 55 years

Total =

See page 143 for the solution!

4 — The number of minutes a soccer game lasted, at the highest altitude

5 — The number of feet Eddie Szula plummeted without a parachute

6 — The number of times Jim McClatchey's heart stopped in one hour

8 — The age of Zhang Huimin when she first ran across China

7 — The height, in feet, of Wave Rock

15 — The length of Leonid Stadnyk's feet in inches

16 — The height, in inches, of Thumbelina

17 — The number of toes on Yassir El Hammud's feet

19 — The amount of feet you can leap on a gravity-defying pogo stick

18 — The number of times Roy C. Sullivan was struck by lightning between 1942 and 1977

INDEX

A

accents, dolphins, 64
Adam, Howard, 111
Adams, John, 123
advertising, in space, 15
aerial ballet, 81
aging disease, 103
Agra, India, 39
air-conditioned jackets, 124
airplanes
  child pulls with hair, 83
  eating, 48
  elderly wing-walker, 112
  jumping over, 77
  pig as passenger, 70
  space plane, 86
airport, refugee lives in transit lounge, 127
Alaska, 90
Albert, Walter, 131
aliens
  in ancient Chinese hieroglyphics, 133
  in Aztec carvings, 132
  Eltanin Antenna, 133
alphabet soup, minuscule, 23
Alps, soccer match on glacier, 24
Amazon basin, 54
American Indian, markings on horse, 136
American presidents, death on Independence
    Day, 123
Amur Bay, Russia, 34
Anderson, R.L., 136
Andes Mountains, 88
Anhui, China, 10
animals
  armadillos, 33
  bears, 90
  buffalo, 69
  calf, 67
  civet cat, 26
  dolphins, 64, 136
  elephants, 13, 60
  fox, 120
  hares, 132
  horses, 55, 56, 66, 136
  hyenas, 68
  monkey, 67
  pandas, 125
  pigs, 55, 67, 70
  porcupines, 65
  rabbits, 57, 64
  racoon, 88
  tigers, 16, 67
  two-headed lamb, 54
  wolves, 89
  zebra/horse hybrid, 66
  see also cats; dogs
Antarctica, giant squid, 57
armadillo races, 33
Armero, Colombia, 90
arms
  bionic, 84
  writing appears on, 120
Armillei, Claudia, 36
Ascoli Piceno, Italy, 36
assault course, 104
astronauts
  in Aztec carvings, 132
  "For Sale" sign on satellites, 15

Atlantic Ocean, 133
ATM machines, dogs use, 71
Aurora, Nebraska, 21
Australia
  cockroach races, 33
  family shares same birthday, 123
  hula-hoop record, 93
  living in caves, 126
  skateboard ride across, 78
  Wave Rock, 11
Austria, floating stage, 13
autism, enormous musical memory, 124
Aztec carvings, of astronauts, 132

B

babies
  crawling marathon, 100
  obese, 102
  septuplets, 101
  very large newborn, 101
  very small newborn, 101
  wigs for, 36
baked beans, lying in bath of, 42
ballet, aerial, 81
balloons
  dinner party suspended below, 25
  inflating with eyes and ears, 109
balls
  ball lightning, 20, 21
  jogging on water, 16
  playing pelota with flaming balls, 44
  of postage stamps, 16
  travelling in ball of steel wire, 16
Bandaloop Dance Company, 81
Baquero, Fernando, 99
Barcelona, Spain, 22
Bath County, Kentucky, 20
Bathini Goud Brothers, 128
Bay Harbor Islands, Florida, 58
beans
  lying in bath of baked beans, 42
  very long green bean, 27
bears, surviving attacks by, 90
Beck, William, 71
beestings, as medicine, 129
bells, bicycle, 41
bicycles
  eating, 48
  fish-shaped, 41
  mini-cycle constructed by foot, 92
billboards
  goalkeeper over motorway, 14
  made of chocolate, 15
  in space, 15
bionic arm, 84
birds
  cat adopts, 64
  drunken pelicans, 65
  four-legged duck, 55
  hang gliding with condors, 88
  image on stone, 10
  mutant feathers, 62
  naked chicken, 63
  pelican wedding, 137
birth, and the number three, 122
birthday, family shares the same, 123
bison, pet, 69
Blaine, David, 17
Blardo, Linda, 122
blind people
  head-butt restores sight, 121
  musical memory, 124

"seeing" with tongue, 108
  waiters in dark restaurant, 125
blood
  green, 130
  hair changes color after transfusion, 131
Blumer, Bob, 8
boat, paper, 13
body art, 107
bodybuilding, for older people, 102
Bölter, Frank, 13
books, smaller than needle's eye, 22
bottles
  balancing matches on, 125
  octopus opens, 60
Bowan, Eli, 98
Brazil
  cat adopts bird, 64
  dog adopts tiger cubs, 67
breathing
  grass growing in lung, 130
  live fish as medicine for, 128
  yogi slows down, 39
Bregenz, Austria, 13
bricks
  breaking on head, 105
  lifting with moustache, 111
Brisbane, Australia, 33
broom, enormous, 23
Bröther, Jürgen, 46
Bucharest, Romania, 22
Buckley, John, 18
budgerigar, mutant feathers, 62
buffalo, pet, 69
buildings
  aerial ballet on, 81
  moving, 19
  piano- and violin-shaped, 14
bullet, embedded in tongue, 90
bun scramble, 44
burping, very loudly, 108

C

Cahaner, Avigdor, 63
calf, pig-like, 67
Cali, Colombia, 100
calligraphy, by child, 82
Calverley, Clifford, 87
Canada
  green blood, 130
  pet buffalo, 69
candles, blowing out with eyes, 109
cans, falling from sky, 20
cardiac arrests
  man drives to funeral home after, 47
  multiple, 46
Carew, Jon-Paul, 131
carp, swan feeds, 66
Carretta, Alf, 112
cars
  child rescues father by lifting, 91
  coffin shaped like, 47
  comic show in, 42
  cricket-bat-shaped, 41
  fox catches head in wheel, 120
  guitar-shaped, 41
  as hanging artwork, 41
  "No Parking" lines, 18
  pulling with ponytail, 111
  rabbit hitches lift in engine, 64
  swimming pool in, 41
cash machines, dogs use, 71
cathedrals, cellists play on roofs of, 39
cats
  adopts bird, 64
  calls emergency services, 65
  cornea transplant from, 85
  extra toes, 64
  fur turns pink, 63
  monkey befriends, 67
  translating calls, 88
  with gold teeth, 63
caves, living in, 126
cellists, play on cathedral rooftops, 39

chainsaws, juggling with, 35
chameleon, very tiny, 57
Chamerel, Mauritius, 10
Charles de Gaulle Airport, Paris, France, 127
Chen Frong-shean, 22
Chen Xiaoyan, 82
chess
  with ice pieces, 44
  youngest grandmaster, 83
Chestnut, Joey, 48
Cheung Chau Island, Hong Kong, 44
chicken
  naked, 63
  small hen lays enormous egg, 57
children
  aging disease, 103
  calligraphy, 82
  climbs Mount Everest, 83
  early developer, 82
  early readers, 83
  lifts car, 91
  long-distance running, 78
  pulls airplane with hair, 83
  pulls train with hair, 83
  radio presenter, 82
  very clever, 83
  writes musical, 82
  youngest chess grandmaster, 83
chimera, woman with two sets of DNA,
    98
China
  beesting therapy, 129
  blowing out candles with eyes, 109
  breaking bricks on head, 105
  building moved, 19
  child runs across, 78
  dog carries shopping, 71
  early readers, 83
  eating glass and porcelain, 92
  grass growing in lung, 130
  Great Wall jumped on skateboard, 86
  hairy rock, 10
  hare symbols, 132
  inflating balloons with eyes, 109
  jogging on water, 16
  mini-cycle made with foot, 92
  panda-dung trinkets, 125
  pelican wedding, 137
  piano- and violin-shaped building, 14
  pigs pull sleds, 70
  porcelain elephant, 13
  robot "clone", 134
  robot police officer, 135
  small hen lays enormous egg, 57
  stone images, 10
  swan feeds fish, 66
  traditional medicine, 128
  two-headed lamb, 54
  two-headed pig, 55
  uncut hair, 110
  uncut nails, 115
  very loud clapping, 109
  walking on knife blades, 38
  weight-lifting, 39
  writing appears on arm, 120
  young calligrapher, 82
chocolate, billboard made of, 15
Chourasia, Ganesh Bhagat, 111
Chukwu, Nkem, 101
churches
  going to in coffin, 47
  symbolic hares in, 132
Ciarciello, Mike, 108
Cimino, Mount, 13
citrus fruit, model of Taj Mahal, 12
civet cat, coffee beans digested by, 26
clapping, very loud, 109
clothing
  air-conditioned jackets, 124
  made from human hair, 110
clouds, parachutists caught in, 21
cockroach races, 33
coffee beans, civet cat digests, 26

coffins
  burial alive in, 46
  car-shaped, 47
  cell phones for, 46
  going to church in, 47
  racing, 33
Coleman, Wendell, 90
Colombia
  baby-crawling marathon, 100
  camp for dogs, 59
  man survives mudslide, 90
comic show, in car, 42
condors, hang gliding with, 88
Constance, Lake, 13
Constantino, 106
Coolidge, Calvin, 88
Coolidge, Grace, 88
Cornthwaite, Dave, 78
corpse, high-altitude tomb, 47
cotton-picker, double-thumbed, 115
Couzzingo, 128
Cowell, Simon, 120
crab-walking, 80
Craven, Janet, 85
Crawford, Emma, 33
crawling marathon, for babies, 100
Crazy Legs Conti, 30
cricket
  bat-shaped car, 41
  hair cut for, 110
Croatia, 48
crockery, elephant made of, 13
Crooks, G.L., 49
cyborgs, marriage to humans, 135

D
Daams, Eddy, 46
Dagg, Henry, 33
Dai Yuequin, 110
dance, aerial, 81
Daniel, J.F., 136
Daredevil Opera Company, 43
d'Arrigo, Angelo, 24, 88
deafness, cured in mountains, 129
death
  in funeral home parking lot, 47
  multiple cardiac arrests, 46
  phoning the dead, 46
Demkina, Natalia, 93
desert, mirror attracts rescue helicopter, 91
Deshler, Nebraska, 23
Dey, Tapan, 114
Diab, Karim, 80
diamond, in dwarf star, 11
dinner parties
  below hot air balloon, 25
  on Mount Everest, 25
dinosaurs, backyard theme park, 33
DNA
  sequences turned into music, 99
  woman with two sets of, 98
dogs
  adopts tiger cubs, 67
  camp for, 59
  carries shopping, 71
  election of footpaths group chairman, 61
  as golf caddy, 71
  heart-shaped pattern on fur, 136
  spa treatments, 58
  starts house fire, 65
  swallows knife, 131
  tennis balls in mouth, 52
  ugliest, 63
  using ATM machines, 71
  walking on hind legs, 60
  wigs for, 58
  with two noses, 54
  yoga for, 68
dolphins
  accents, 64
  artificial tail, 136
drilling holes through hair, 111
Dropa Stones, 133

Drossel, Arnd, 16
drunken pelicans, 65
duck, four-legged, 55
dunes, multi-colored, 10
dung, panda-dung trinkets, 125
dwarf star, diamond core, 11

E
ears
  glass cup in hole in lobe, 106
  inflating balloons with, 109
  long hair growing from, 110
  pulling train with, 92
  silicone implants, 85
  weight lifting with, 39
earth, multi-colored, 10
Easter Island, language, 133
Edinburgh, Scotland, 42
eggs
  frying with solar power, 33
  small hen lays enormous egg, 57
Egyptian hieroglyphs, helicopters and
    submarines in, 132
El Hammud, Yassir, 115
Elbe, River, 34
elephants
  made of crockery, 13
  paintings by, 60
Ellis, Shaun, 89
Eltanin Antenna, 133
emergency services, cat calls, 65
England
  ball lightning, 20
  cellists play on cathedral rooftops, 39
  chocolate billboard, 15
  dogs use ATM machines, 71
  elderly wing-walker, 112
  four-legged duck, 55
  giant leek, 26
  giant Scrabble® board, 45
  glockenspiel fence, 33
  Great Fire of London re-enacted, 19
  hitch-hiking rabbit, 64
  huge bag of fries, 27
  "No Parking" lines, 18
  pink cat, 63
  shark embedded in roof, 18
  theater in public restroom, 32
  theme park in backyard, 33
  Tough Guy Challenge, 104
The Enigma, 107
Ernst, Jarislav, 85
Everest, Mount
  child climbs, 83
  dinner party on, 25
  fatalities on, 113
  hang glider flies over, 24
  microlight flies over, 21
  oldest climber, 113
  paraglider ascends, 24
  race on, 78
expressions, on robot's face, 134
extreme ironing, 37
eyes
  blowing out candles with, 109
  cornea transplanted from cat's eye, 85
  inflating balloons with, 109
  popping out of socket, 108
  weight-lifting with eyelids, 39
  X-ray vision, 93

F
facial expressions, robots, 134
feathers
  mutant budgerigar, 62
  naked chicken, 63
feet
  extra toes, 115
  legless man, 98
  mini-cycle constructed by foot, 92
  walking with heels twisted forwards, 109
fence, as glockenspiel, 33
fingernails, uncut, 115

fingers, extra, 115
fires
  dog starts, 65
  Great Fire of London re-enacted, 19
fish
  bicycle shaped like, 41
  live fish as medicine, 128
  playing soccer, 61
  swan feeds, 66
Flexman, Alana, 130
flight
  one-man hovercraft, 86
  with rocket belt and jetpack, 87
fly, robotic, 134
food, analyzing every meal, 49
Fore, Amia, 121
Fort Worth, Texas, 33
fox, catches head in car wheel, 120
France
  horse/zebra hybrid, 66
  refugee lives in airport lounge, 127
Fraser, Billy, 102
French fries, huge bag of, 27
friends, reunited after 60 years, 123
funeral home, man drives to after heart
    attack, 47
funerals, going to funerals of complete
    strangers, 47
fungus, hairy rock, 10
furniture, oversized, 23
Fuzhou, China, 137

G
Gandhi, Bitu, 109
Gardner, Dale, 15
Gatlinburg, Tennessee, 49
Germany
  cell phones for coffins, 46
  extreme ironing, 37
  fish-shaped bicycle, 41
  giant billboard, 14
  high-wire stunts on motorcycles, 87
  mud-olympics, 34
  oversized furniture, 23
  paper boat, 13
  parachutists caught in cloud, 21
  pencil in head, 131
  traveling in ball of steel wire, 16
Gill, Zafar, 39
glacier, soccer match on, 24
glass
  ball lightning passes through, 21
  eating, 92
  glockenspiel, fence as, 33
Glover, Derek, 129
gold teeth, cat with, 63
golf caddy, dog as, 71
Gomez, Jose, 12
grandchild, face appears on kneecap, 121
grass, growing in lung, 130
grasshoppers, jumping ability, 137
Gray, Chadwick, 107
Great Torrington, England, 19
Great Wall of China, leaping over on
    skateboard, 86
Greece, Ancient, 133
green bean, very long, 27
Grylls, Bear, 24, 25
guitar-shaped car, 41
Gunnarson, Dean, 74
Gupta, Anil, 106
gyroscope, spinning inside, 17

H
Habu the Iron-Tongued Man, 105
Hai Ngoc, 108
hailstones, enormous, 21
hair
  changes color after blood transfusion, 131
  child pulls airplane with, 83
  child pulls train with, 83
  clothing made from, 110
  cricket-match hair cut, 110

drilling holes through, 111
  hairy rock, 10
  lifting bricks with moustache, 111
  long hair growing from ears, 110
  never cut, 110
  pulling cars with, 111
  tattoos hidden by, 133
  threading hair through, 111
  wigs for babies, 36
  wigs for dogs, 58
  writing with pen clipped to, 114
Halcrow, Lucy and Georgia, 83
hands
  double-thumbed cotton-picker, 115
  extra fingers, 115
hang gliding
  flying over Mount Everest, 24
  with condors, 88
Hanks, Tom, 127
Harbin, China, 57
hares, symbols found in churches, 132
hats, wizards', 132
Hayward, Julie, 62
head
  balancing on jaw, 115
  breaking bricks on, 105
  burying in sand, 39
  exploding head stunt, 43
  horns implanted in, 107
  pencil in, 131
  on plates, 48
  transplants, 84
  two-headed lamb, 54
  two-headed pig, 55
head-butt restores sight, 121
Headington, England, 18
heart attacks
  man drives to funeral home after,
    47
  multiple, 46
heart rate, slowing down, 39
heart-shaped pattern on fur, 136
Heine, Bill, 18
helicopters
  in Egyptian hieroglyphs, 132
  mirror attracts rescuers, 91
Hereford, England, 27
hieroglyphics
  Easter Island script, 133
  helicopters and submarines in,
    132
  records of aliens in, 133
high-wire stunts, 87
Himalayas, 133
Hodgson, Kylee, 100
Hogg, Mark, 49
Holmes, Michael, 91
Hong Kong, bun scramble, 11
horns, implanted in head, 107
horses
  horse/zebra hybrid, 66
  miniature, 56
  tallest, 56
  two-legged, 55
  unusual markings, 136
hot dogs, speed-eating, 48
house, shark embedded in roof, 18
hovercraft, one-man, 86
hula hoops, spinning multiple, 93
Hungary, woman survives in icy lake, 91
Hunn, Paul, 108
Hurley, Harry, 27
hybrid, horse/zebra, 66
hyenas, as pets, 68

I
ice
  chess pieces, 44
  holding onto with teeth, 91
  leaping between ice floes, 34
  swimming in icy water, 80
Independence Day, American
    presidents die on, 123

India
  burying head in sand, 39
  cricket-bat-shaped car, 41
  cricket-match haircut, 110
  lifting bricks with moustache, 111
  live fish as medicine, 128
  man run over by tractor, 104
  model of Taj Mahal, 12
  red rain, 21
  very long ear hair, 110
  walking with heels twisted forwards, 109
  writing with pen clipped to hair, 114
Indonesia
  civet cat coffee, 26
  man survives tsunami, 90
insects
  cockroach races, 33
  in Popsicles, 26
  Robo-Fly, 134
ironing, extreme, 37
Isaac, Gerwyn, 106
Israel, naked chicken, 63
Italy
  rocking stone, 13
  very long wedding veil, 36

J
jackets, air-conditioned, 124
Janaway, Nicky, 55
Japan
  air-conditioned jackets, 124
  cat calls translated, 88
  dog walks on hind legs, 60
  dog with heart shape on coat, 136
  dolphin with artificial tail, 136
  fish play soccer, 61
  paper lantern festival, 46
  robot with facial expressions, 134
  soldier found 28 years after war ends, 126
  spa treatments for dogs, 58
  yoga for dogs, 68
jaw, balancing on, 115
Jefferson, Thomas, 123
jet engines
  flight with jetpack, 87
  jet-powered skateboard, 76
jigsaw puzzle, tattooed over entire body, 107
jogging
  long-distance run by child, 78
  running marathon in rhinoceros suit, 79
  on water, 16
juggling, with chainsaws, 35
jumping, grasshoppers' ability, 137
Jungfrau Glacier, 24

K
Kahn, Oliver, 14
Kaifeng, China, 105
Karjakin, Sergey, 83
Karkoss, Don, 121
Ke Kuaile, 55
Kearney, Michael, 82
Keegan, Karen, 98
Keokuk, Iowa, 20
Khalina, Tatyana, 101
Khlebnikov, Bruce, 83
King, Joel, 76
kneecap, grandchild's face appears on, 121
Knievel, Robbie, 77
knives
  dog swallows, 131
  standing barefoot on blades, 38
Kobayashi, Takeru, 48
Krull, Richard, 99
Kuala Lumpur, Malaysia, 92

L
Lackey, Tom, 112
lamb, two-headed, 54

languages
  Easter Island, 133
  unknown language in manuscript, 132
lantern festival, 46
leek, enormous, 26
legs
  four-legged duck, 55
  legless man, 98
  legless woman, 98
  two-legged pony, 55
lemons, model of Taj Mahal, 12
Leonardo da Vinci, 106
letters, minuscule alphabet soup, 23
Levy, David, 135
Li Jianping, 115
lightbulbs, walking barefoot over, 38
Lightcap, Dick, 125
lightning
  ball lightning, 20, 21
  surviving multiple strikes, 91
Liverpool Cathedral, England, 39
lobster, wallet found in claws, 123
London
  chocolate billboard, 15
  giant Scrabble® board, 45
  Great Fire re-enacted 19
  marathon in rhinoceros suit, 79
  "No Parking" lines, 18
Lorincz, Adam, 82
Los Angeles, 65, 82
Lotito, Michel, 48
loud noises
  burping, 108
  clapping, 109
lung, grass growing in, 130

M
McAdam, Lon, 91
McClatchey, Jim, 46
McGowan, Mark, 42
MacInnes, Scott, 90
Madagascar, 57
Malawi, 57
Malaysia, 92
Manitou Springs, Colorado, 33
manuscript, in unknown language, 132
marathons, wearing rhinoceros suit, 79
marriage, cyborg/human, 135
matches, balanced on bottle, 125
Mauritius, 10
meat, falling from sky, 20
medicine
  bee stings as, 129
  live fish as, 128
  traditional Chinese, 128
Meredith-Hardy, Richard, 24
metal, eating, 48
Mexico
  cornea transplanted from cat's eye, 85
  pelota with flaming ball, 44
Michigan, Lake, 21
microlight, flies over Mount Everest, 24
Miller, Fred W., 16
Ming, Benji, 42
mirror, attracts rescue helicopter, 91
Mitama Festival, Japan, 46
Mitchell, Claudia, 84
Mongolia, ancient tomb, 47
monkey, befriends cat, 67
Monroe, James, 123
Moriarty, Richard, 41
Morris, Eric, 104
Moscow, Russia, 77, 80, 83
motorcycles, high-wire stunts, 87
mountains
  child climbs Mount Everest, 83
  coffin slides down side of, 33
  deafness cured on, 129
  dinner party on Mount Everest, 25
  high-altitude tomb, 47
  oldest climber of Mount Everest, 113
  paraglider ascends Mount Everest, 24
  race on Mount Everest, 78

moustache, lifting bricks with, 111
mud
  man rescued from mudslide, 90
  mud-olympics, 34
  mudpacks for dogs, 58
Munoz, Annie, 26
muscles, bionic arm, 84
music
  child writes musical, 82
  DNA sequences turned into, 99
  enormous memory for, 124
  very old rock band, 112
musical instruments
  building shaped like, 14
  cellists play on cathedral rooftops, 39
  glockenspiel fence, 33

N
Nahyan, Sheikh Hamad Bin Hamdan Al, 40
Nakamatsu, Yoshiro, 49
Nasseri, Mehran Karimi, 127
Neale, Dennis, 32
New York
  body art, 107
  hot-dog eating contest, 48
  marathon in rhinoceros suit, 79
  spinning inside gyroscope, 17
New Zealand
  clever sisters, 83
  mutant budgerigar, 62
  octopus opens bottles, 60
Niagara Falls
  going over in barrel, 35
  tightrope walking across, 87
Nicholson, Chelsea, 57
Noble, Samantha, 122
North Pole, swimming at, 80
noses, dog with two, 54
numbers, birth and the number three, 122

O
Oates, Kareena, 93
Oatman, Arizona, 33
octopuses
  opens bottles, 60
  wrestling with, 104
octuplets, 101
Ohrberg, Jay, 41
Okinawa, Japan, 136
opera, on floating stage, 13
oranges, model of Taj Mahal, 12
oysters, eating large quantities of, 49

P
paintings
  body art, 107
  by elephants, 60
  longest, 22
  as tattoos, 106
Panama City, 26
panda-dung trinkets, 125
paper boat, 13
paper lantern festival, 46
parachutists
  caught in cloud, 21
  lands in blackberry bush, 91
  parachute fails to open, 120
Paravichini, Derek, 124
pelicans
  drunken, 65
  wedding, 137
pelota, 44
pen, writing with pen clipped to hair, 114
pencil, in head, 131
Perez, Kimberley, 82
Phipps, Jean, 125
piano, building shaped like, 14
pigs
  as aircraft passenger, 70
  calf-like, 67
  pulling sleds, 70
  two-headed, 55
Pilot, Will, 80

pogo stick, very high bounce on, 76
poison, porcupines drink prussic acid, 65
Poland, tongue reconstruction, 85
police
  cat phones for, 65
  robotic, 135
Polo, "Little Giant" Eddie, 111
pony, two-legged, 55
ponytails, pulling weights with, 83, 111
popcorn eating, 30
Popsicles, worms in, 26
porcelain
  eating, 92
  elephant made of, 13
porcupines, drinking prussic acid, 65
postage stamps, enormous ball of, 16
potatoes, huge bag of French fries, 27
presidents, death on Independence Day, 123
Primo, Efrain Gómez, 90
prussic acid, porcupines drink, 65
public restroom, theater in, 32
Pugh, Lewis, 80
pulse, slowing down, 39
puppet theater, in public restroom, 32

R
rabbits
  giant, 57
  hitches lift in car engine, 64
racoon, White House pet, 88
radio presenter, child, 82
raft, man survives on, 90
rain, red, 21
refugee, lives in transit lounge, 127
Regina, Ruth, 58
reptiles, very tiny, 57
restaurants, dining in the dark, 125
restroom, theater in, 32
rhinoceros suit, running marathon in, 79
ribs, DIY surgery, 128
rings, long-lost, 122
river, crossing on single bamboo stick, 76
robots
  cyborg/human marriages, 135
  facial expressions, 134
  personal "clone", 134
  police, 135
  Robo-Fly, 134
rock band, very old, 112
rockets
  advertising on, 15
  flight with rocket belt, 87
rocks
  hairy, 10
  rocking stone, 13
  Wave Rock, Australia, 11
Rodriguez, Epigmegnia, 85
roller-skating, twins have accidents, 123
Romania, very long painting, 22
rooster, image on stone, 10
Rosheisen, Gary, 65
Rubik's Cube, 45
Rudolph, Amelia, 81
Russia
  boy pulls child airplane with hair, 83
  ice chess pieces, 44
  leaping between ice floes, 34
  snowmobile, 77
  swimming in icy river, 80

S
Saber, Harold, 47
St. Greathouse, L., 55
San Francisco, most crooked street, 18
Sanchez Souza, Aurora, 99
Sandberg, Colt, 43
Sanville, Franks, 67
Sarder, Bhola, 110
satellites, for sale, 15
Sautner, Jim and Linda, 69
Scarola, Jane, 131
Schill, Jeremy and Rique, 91
Scotland, comic show in car, 42

Scott, Eric, 87
Scrabble®, giant board, 45
sculpture, car as, 41
Senft, Didi, 41
septuplets, 101
Seurat, Georges, 106
Shahputra, Rizal, 90
sharks
    embedded in roof, 18
    large pregnancy, 65
Shaw, Phil, 37
shoes
    enormous, 99
    soccer team on sneakers, 22
shopping, dog carries, 71
shrimp, shower of, 20
Shwaykani, Faten and Noureddin, 68
Siberia, 101
Siggins, Rose, 98
Simpson, Andrew, 33
Singh, Jagga, 104
skateboards
    crossing Australia on, 78
    jet-powered, 76
    leaping Great Wall of China on, 86
skin, writing appears on arm, 120
skydiver, lands in blackberry bush, 91
sleds, pigs pulling, 70
sleep
    growth during, 109
    long time without, 108
sneakers, soccer team on, 22
snowmobile, 77
soccer
    fish playing, 61
    on glacier, 24
    goalkeeper billboard over motorway,
      14
    team on sneakers, 22
soft-drink cans, falling from sky, 20
solar power, frying eggs with, 33
soldier, found 28 years after war ends, 126
Soledad, Mount, 20
soup, minuscule alphabet, 23
spa treatments, for dogs, 58
space plane, 86
Spain, going to church in coffin, 47
Sparre, Nina, 110
Spector, Laura, 107
speed-eating, hot dogs, 48
splits, crossing river while doing, 76
squid, enormous, 57
Stadnyk, Leonid, 99
stage, floating, 13
Stamp, Danielle, 118
stamps, enormous ball of, 16
star, diamond core, 11
Star Trek, 130
Steele, David, 63
Steindl family, 123
stings, as medicine, 129
stones
    image of rooster on, 10
    rocking, 13
street, most crooked, 18
Strenkert, Zack, 102
Stuart, "Sledneck" Lee, 77
Stubblefield, R.L., 115
student, very young, 82
submarines, in Egyptian hieroglyphs, 132
Sullivan, Roy C., 91
Superstition Wilderness, Arizona, 91
surgery
    DIY, 128
    patient with green blood, 130
swan, feeds fish, 66
swimming
    in icy river, 80
    at North Pole, 80
swimming pool, in car, 41
Swisshelm, Helen, 122
Syria, 68
Szula, Eddie, 120

T
Tachi, Satoe, 68
Tacket, John, 103
tails, artificial tail for dolphin, 136
Taiwan, 22
Taj Mahal, citrus fruit model, 12
tattoos
    on back, 106
    hidden by hair, 133
    jigsaw-puzzle tattoo over entire body, 107
    old-master reproductions, 106
Taylor, Amillia Sonja, 101
Taylor, Annie Edson, 35
Taylor, Dorothy, 125
teeth
    cat with gold teeth, 63
    holding onto ice with, 91
    pulling train with, 92
telephones, phoning the dead, 46
televisions, eating, 48
Temba Tsheri, 83
Terry, Jaqueline, 115
Tewkesbury, England, 20
Thailand
    elephant paintings, 60
    monkey befriends cat, 67
theaters
    comic show in car, 42
    floating stage, 13
    in public restroom, 32
theme park, in backyard, 33
Thiel, Paul, 122
Thomas, Alison, 64
Thompson, J.M., 111
Thompson, Jalisa Mae, 108
Thumbelina, 56
thumbs, double-thumbed cotton-picker, 115
thunderstorm, parachutists caught in cloud, 21
tigers
    dog adopts cubs, 67
    man in steel ball in cage of, 16
tightrope walking, 87
toes, extra, 64, 115
Tokyo, Japan, 46, 58
tomb, high-altitude, 47
tongue
    bullet embedded in, 90
    rolling into shapes, 96
    "seeing" with, 108
    transplant, 85
    weight lifting with, 105
tornados, 20
tourism, in space, 86
tower, bun scramble up, 44
Traber, Johann Sr. and Jr., 87
tractor, being run over by, 104
trailer home, very large, 40
trains
    child pulls with hair, 83
    pulling with ears, 92
    pulling with teeth, 92
transit lounge, refugee lives in, 127
transplants
    cornea from cat's eye, 85
    head, 84
    tongue, 85
trucks
    enormous, 40
    very large convoy, 40
    very small, 40
tsunami, man survives on raft, 90
twins
    of different color, 100
    early readers, 83
    roller-skating accidents, 123
Tyagi, B.D., 110

U
Ukraine, very tall man, 99
underwater
    extreme ironing, 37
    mysterious structure, 133
United Arab Emirates, 40

University of California at Los Angeles, 23

V
veil, very long, 36
Velu, Kathakrishnan, 92
village, in cave, 126
violin, building shaped like, 14
volcanic eruption, rescued from mudslide, 90
Voynich Manuscript, 132

W
Wales
    cat with extra toes, 64
    dolphin accents, 64
wallets
    found in lobster's claws, 123
    long-lost, 122
Wang Chengke, 92
water, jogging on, 16
watermelon, exploding head stunt, 43
Wave Rock, Australia, 11
Way, Danny, 86
webs, mysterious fall of, 21
weddings
    for pelicans, 137
    very long veil, 36
Wegner, Margret, 131
weight lifting
    lifting bricks with moustache, 111
    with ear, 39
    with eyelids, 39
    with tongue, 105
Welling, Carrie, 125
Wembley Stadium, London, 45
Wessels, Georg, 99
Westlake, Paul, 123
wheel, fox catches head in, 120
Wiese, Cassidy and Marissa, 123
wigs
    for babies, 36
    for dogs, 58
Williams, Alan, 27
Wilson, Billy, 104
wing-walking, 112
Wisconsin, 21
wizards, hats, 132
wolves, living with, 89
worms
    eating, 49
    in Popsicles, 26
Worth, Philip and Joan, 63
wrestling, with octopuses, 104
writing
    appears on arm, 120
    pen clipped to hair, 114
Wuhan, China, 135
Wuzhou, China, 19

X
X-ray vision, 93

Y
Yadav, Sudhakar, 41
Yanagisawa, Katsusuke, 113
Yarde, Abbey, 26
yoga, canine, 68
yogis, 39
Yokoi, Shoichi, 126
Yu Hongqua, 109

Z
zebra/horse hybrid, 66
Zhang Huimin, 78
Zhang Quan, 109
Zhang Xinquan, 92
Zhang Yingmin, 109
Zhuang Zefang, 83
Zhuang Zezheng, 83
The Zimmers, 112
Zoltany, Ani, 91
Zorchak, Nathan, 35
zorse (horse/zebra hybrid), 66
Zou Renti, 134

ANSWERS

Pages 72–73

1. B, Elephant.
2. C, 4. The common garden slug also has 27,000 teeth.
3. D, all of the above. Starfish do have at the end of each arm a small eyespot, which senses light, but which is not sophisticated enough to see images as we do.
4. D, Funnel web spider. The males are more dangerous than the females. The venom is most deadly to humans. Other mammals like cats and dogs are more resistant to their poison.
5. C, 3. It has one to pump blood through its body, and two to pump blood through each of its two gills.
6. D, 80. The sloth is also the slowest mammal on Earth, moving at only six feet per minute, so it's not an action-packed animal.
7. D, Sea-cucumbers. If disturbed, they throw up—ejecting not only feces, but also particles of decayed food and mud over their attacker. The slimy discharge contains much of their guts, which look like pale threads.
8. D, Bulldog ant. It stings and bites at the same time and has killed humans.
9. B, Oyster. Oysters are able to change from male to female and back again, depending on which is best for mating.
10. C, Ribbon worm. In the late 1800s, a ribbon worm measuring 180 feet was washed up on the shore of Scotland.
11. B, Bird. Cave swiftlets of Southeast Asia nest in the ceilings of great caverns. They make their nests from their own saliva, or spit, which dries as a glassy solidified goo, glued to the cavern rock. People use ladders to reach and collect the nests, which are made into the culinary delicacy bird's nest soup. The essence of this dish is therefore swiftlet spit!
12. C, Hippopotamus. Well, not really. A hippo's skin sweats an oily red fluid to keep the skin healthy. People used to think that hippos sweated blood!
13. B, Lizard. The glass lizard has no legs, and at times no tail! The tail breaks off and wriggles as a decoy if attacked.
14. D, 2,200. The tiny frogs are only the size of a man's thumbnail – that's about one inch long!
15. D, 500 volts. The electric eel delivers 500-plus volts, enough to knock out a horse or kill a person.
16. D, Rhinoceros beetle. It can lift 850 times its own weight.
17. B, Common fly. On average, the common fly's life expectancy can be anything from 17 to 20 days.
18. A, Viperfish. The viperfish uses them to attract fish in the dark depths where it hunts. Its dorsal fin has a light-producing tip to lure fish in!
19. B, Stonefish. In its dorsal fin it has 13 stout spines, which inject its venom, causing intense pain and potentially killing its victims.
20. A, Ostrich. Their eyes weigh two ounces, and their brains only 1½ ounces. They also have three eyelids.

Pages 138–139

$10,000 \div 10 + 990 + 10 - 2,000 + 50 + 45 \times 8 \times 2 + 26 + 34 + 71 + (6 \times 60) + 17 - 17 - 11 + 7 + 5 - 3 = \mathbf{2009}$ (the year of this Special Edition!)

PHOTO CREDITS: Ripley Entertainment Inc. and the editors of this book wish to thank the following photographers, agents, and other individuals for permission to use and reprint the following photographs in this book. Any photographs included in this book that are not acknowledged below are property of the Ripley Archives and MKP Archives. Great effort has been made to obtain permission from the owners of all materials included in this book. Any errors that may have been made are unintentional and will gladly be corrected in future printings if notice is sent to Ripley Entertainment, Inc., 7576 Kingspointe Parkway, Suite 188, Orlando, Florida 32819.

COVER/TITLE PAGE: Lizardman, Courtesy of Erik Sprague

BACK COVER: Mr. Mangetout—©Nils Jorgensen/Rex USA; Everest dinner—Courtesy of "The Formal Diners": Henry Shelford, Tom Shelford, Rob Sully, Caio Buzzolini, Josh Heming, Nakul Pathak, Robbie Aitken; Elwood Ugly Dog—©A. Miller/WENN/Newscom

PAGE 4: Ripley Archives

PAGE 5: Ripley Archives

PAGE 6: Dogs at ATM—George S. Blonsky/Canine Partners; Skateboard—Richard Eaton

PAGE 7: Ripley Archives

Chapter 1: 8: Toastmobile—George Whiteside; **10:** Hairy Rock—Yang Fan/ChinaFotoPress/Photocome/PA Photos; Colored Earth—World Pictures/Photoshot; Rooster Stone—Xie Zhengyi/ChinaFotoPress/Photocome/PA Photos; **11:** Solid Surf—Steve Vidler/Dinodia Photo Library; **12:** Lemon Building—Reuters/Eric Gaillard; **13:** Skeleton Stage—Action Press/Rex Features; Plate Elephant—UPPA/Photoshot; Paper Boat—Reuters/Christian Charisius; **14–15:** Adidas Bridge—Courtesy of Adidas; **14:** Musical Building—Zhang Anhao/Photocome/PA Photos; **15:** Nasa "For Sale"—Corbis; Chocolate Billboard—Paul Grover/Rex Features; **16:** Ball with Tigers—Oliver Krato/DPA/PA Photos; Water Balls—Sipa Press/Rex Features; **17:** David Blaine—Charles Sykes/Rex Features; **18:** Crooked Street—Ron Watts/Corbis; Yellow Line—Jonathan Hordle/Rex Features; Shark Roof—Tim Graham/Getty Images; **19:** Pudding Lane on Fire—Julian Makey/Rex Features; Pudding Lane—Great Torrington Cavaliers; **20:** Shrimps—Daniel Sainthorant/Fotolia; **22:** Tiny Book—Reuters/Simon Kwong; Painting—Reuters/Mihai Barbu; Soccer Shoes—Reuters/Gustau Nacarino; **23:** Horses—AP/Jens Meyer; **24:** Mountain Football—Reuters/Christian Hartmann; Bear Grylls—Camera Press/Martin Pope; **25:** Mountain Dining—Camera Press/ED/JM; **26:** Big Leek—Carl De Souza/Rex Features; Insect Lolly—Reuters/Alberto Lowe; Cat Coffee—AP/Bullit Marquez; **27:** Big Bag of Chips—Lewis Whyld/Rex Features

Chapter 2: 30: Popcorn—Erik C Pendzich/Rex Features; **32:** Toilet Theatre—Daniel Graves/Rex Features; **33:** Musical Fence—Simon Jones/Rex Features; Jurassic Park—Keith Meatheringham/Rex Features; Coffin Racing—Andra DuRee Martin; **34:** Ice Jumping—Camera Press/Itar-Tass/Vladirmir Sayapin; Mud Football—Reuters/Morris MacMatzen; **35:** Chainsaw Juggling—Roger Bamber/Rex Features; **36:** Bride with Long Train—Action Press/Rex Features; Baby Wigs—Rex Features; **37:** Extreme Ironing—Rex Features; **38:** Walking on Light Bulbs—Camera Press/Dong Jinling/Phototex; **39:** Lifting Bucket with Eyes—Camera Press/Dong Jinling/Phototex; Yogi—Fortean/Aarsleff/TopFoto; Cellists—Camera Press/Don McPhee/Guardian; **40:** Big Truck—Andy Wilman/Rex Features; **41:** Guitar Limo—Camera Press/Gamma/Sander Eric Mercedes 450SL by Jay Ohrberg; Fish Vehicle—Reuters/Tobias Schwarz; Cricket Bat Car—Reuters/Stringer India; **42:** Car Theater—Rex Features; Breakfast Bath—Nils Jorgensen/Rex Features; **43:** Watermelons—Reuters/Will Burgess WB/JJ; **44:** Fire Football—Reuters/Henry Romero; Ice Chess—Natalia Kolesnikova/AFP/Getty Images; Bun Run—Reuters/Bobby Yip; **45:** Scrabble—Richard Gardner/Rex Features; **46:** Lanterns—Radu Razvan/Fotolia; **47:** Coffin Festival—Reuters/Miguel Vidal; Mountain—Dmitry Pichugin/Fotolia; **48:** Eating Hot Dogs—Kristin Callahan/Rex Features; Food Parade—Reuters/Nikola Solic; Metal Eater—¬Nils Jorgensen/Rex Features

Chapter 3: 54: Two Headed Sheep—Cao Zheizheng/Phototex, Camera Press; **55:** Duck—Barry Batchelor/PA Wire/PA Photos; Two Headed Pig—Reuters/China Daily Information Corp – CDIC; **56:** Dog and Pony—Austin Hargrave/Barcroft Media; **57:** Giant Rabbit—Phil Yeomans/Rex Features; Giant Squid—Getty Images; Pygmy Chameleon—Reuters/Matko Biljak; **58:** Dog Wig—Joe Raedle/Getty Images; Pampered Dog—Haruyoshi Yamaguchi/Corbis; **59:** Dog Camp—Jose Gomez; **60:** Painting Elephant—Reuters/Sukree Sukplang; Octopus—Reuters/Stringer New Zealand; Poodle—Koichi Kamoshida/Getty Images; **61:** Football Fish—Reuters/Toshiyuki Aizawa; **62:** Budgerigar—Rex Features; **63:** Featherless Chicken—Sipa Press/Rex Features; Ugly Dog—Ben Margot/AP/PA Photos; Pink Cat—Barry Batchelor/PA Archive/PA Photos; **65:** Doughnut—Olga Hasan/Fotolia; **66:** Zorse—Alain Julien/Stringer/Getty Images; **67:** Monkey and Cat—Reuters/Sukree Sukplang; Dog and Tiger—Reuters/Stringer Brazil; **68:** Dog Yoga—Reuters/Kiyoshi Ota; Hyena—Reuters/Khaled Al Hariri; **69:** Buffalo—Carlo Allegri/Getty Images; **70:** Ski Resort Pig—BJCB/Guo Tieliu/Photocome/Newscom; **71:** Dog at Market—Wang Hu/ChinaFotoPress/Photocome/PA Photos; ATM Dogs—George S. Blonsky/Canine Partners

Chapter 4: 74: Escape Artist—Ken Hart; **76:** Bamboo Canoe—Camera Press/Qin Gang/ChinaFotoPress; Pogo Stick—Camera Press/Clare Boughey; Skateboard—Richard Eaton; **77:** Snowmobile—Camera Press/Itar-Tass; **78:** Running Girl—Reuters/China Daily Information Corp – CDIC; Skater Boy—Holly Allen/Rex Features; Everest Marathon—Reuters/STR New; **79:** Rhino Racing—Benny Snyder/AP/PA Photos; **80:** Arctic Swim—Reuters/Ho New; Water Endurance—Camera Press/Itar-Tass/Konstantin Postnikov; **81:** Bandaloop Dancers—Paul A. Souders/Corbis; **82:** Girl Writing—Camera Press/Gamma/Xinhua-Chine Nouvelle; **83:** Girl Reading—Camera Press/Xinhua; Mount Everest—QiangBa DanZhen/Fotolia; **84:** Bionic Arm—Reuters/Jason Reed; **85:** Silicone Ear—Gareth Copley/PA Archive/PA Photos; Hairy Tongue—De Ville/Rex Features; **86:** Flying Saucer—Moller International; Skateboard—Reuters/Jason Lee; Space Tourism—Reuters/Ho New; **87:** High Wire—Timm Schamberger/Getty Images; **88:** Cat Translator—AFP/Getty Images/Toru Yamanaka; Anglo d'Arrigo-G/N, Camera Press; **89:** Man with Wolves—Linda Cowen/Wolfpack Management; **90:** Mud Slide—Mauro Carraro/Rex Features; **91:** Mountain—Elemental Imaging/Fotolia; **92:** Glass Eater—CN Imaging/Photoshot; Bike Assembled with Feet—Reuters/Nir Elias; Man Pulling Train—Vincent Thain/AP/PA Photos; **93:** Hula Hooping—Samantha Sin/Stringer/AFP/Getty Images

Chapter 5: 96: Tongue Twister—Manichi Rafi; **98:** Double Helix—ktsdesign/Fotolia; Half Woman—Incredible Features/Barcroft Media; **99:** Big Shoes—Reuters/Stringer Russia; **100:** Twins—worldwidefeatures.com; **101:** Big Baby—Reuters/Stringer Russia; Tiny Baby—Reuters/Ho New; Octuplets—F. Carter Smith/Sygma/Corbis; **102:** Body Builder—Allover Denmark/Rex Features; Big Toddler—Tim Roske/AP/PA Photos; **103:** Mr Tacket—Gerald Herbert/AP/PA Photos; **104:** Tractor—AFP/Getty Images; Tough Guy—Reuters/Darren Staples; **105:** Bricks—Reuters/China Daily Information Corp – CDIC; **106:** Tattoo—Anil Gupta/Inkline Studio, NYC; Glass in Earlobe—Reuters/Jorge Silva; Lizardman, Courtesy of Erik Sprague; **107:** Body Painting—Beth A. Keiser/AP/PA Photos; **109:** Balloons—Skip Odonnell/iStockphoto; Clapping Hands—Cemanoliso/Fotolia; **110:** Ear Hair—Prakash Hatvalne/AP/PA Photos; Long Hair—ChinaFotoPress/Pan Lianggan/Photocome/PA Photos; Cricket Hair—Deshakalyan Chowdhury/AFP/Getty Images; **111:** Strong Beard—Sourav/Stringer/AFP/Getty Images; **112:** The Zimmers—Copyright 2007 X-Phonics Music; Wing Walker—Mary Turner/Rex Features; **113:** Everest—Hiro YAmagata/AFP/Getty Images; **114:** Writing with Hair—Sourav/Stringer/AFP/Getty Images; **115:** Six Fingers—Peter Bischoff/Barcroft Media; Long Nails—Camera Press/Top Photo

Chapter 6: 120: Fox Stuck in Tyre—Solent News/Rex Features; Good Luck—Camera Press/Fei Qiang/Phototex; **121:** Knee Babies—Amia Fore; **122:** Clock—Volodymyr Vasylkiv/Fotolia; Lost Wallet—Bill Greenblatt/Newscom/Photoshot; **124:** Shirt—Reuters/Michael Caronna; **125:** Restaurant—Reuters/Jason Redmond; Panda Poo—Reuters/China Daily Information Corp – CDIC; **126:** Japanese Man—Keystone/Getty Images; Cave Homes—Brendan Beirne/Rex Features; **127:** Terminal Man—Christophe Calais/Corbis; **128:** Facial Paralysis Cure—Reuters/Stringer Shanghai; Live Fish—Reuters/Stringer India; **129:** Bee Sting Therapy—Reuters/China Daily Information Corp – CDIC; **130:** Mr Spock—NBCU Photo Bank/Rex Features; **131:** Pencil—Studioxil/Fotolia; **132:** Wizard Hat—Bobbie Osborne/iStockphoto; **133:** Alien Visit—Lee Pettet/iStockphoto; Island Script—John Snelgrove/iStockphoto; **134:** Robot Expressions—Reuters/Yuriko Nakao; Robot Clone—Reuters/Jason Lee; Robo-Fly—SWNS/Rex Features; **135:** Robo-cop—Reuters/China Daily Information Corp – CDIC; **136:** Dolphin—Reuters/Yuriko Nakao; Dog—Reuters/Issei Kato; **137:** Pelicans—Reuters/China Daily Information Corp - CDIC